EMPOWERING MINDS: NEW HORIZONS IN EDUCATION

DR. FRANCES KETAN VAIDYA

Made with ♥ on the Notion Press Platform
www.notionpress.com

SHREE LALLAN TIWARI, FOUNDER CHAIRMAN, RAHUL EDUCATION SOCIETY

This book is dedicated to Shri Lallan R. Tiwari, the esteemed founder member of the Rahul Education Society. His unwavering vision and commitment to the principle of "Education for All" have inspired countless individuals and transformed lives. His passion for empowering educators and learners alike serves as a guiding light in our collective journey toward inclusive and holistic education. May his legacy continue to inspire future generations to embrace the transformative power of knowledge

UTSAV RAHUL TIWARI -CHIEF OPERATING OFFICER, RAHUL EDUCATION

This book is also dedicated to Mr. Utsav Rahul Tiwari, Chief Operating Officer, Rahul Education Society whose unwavering motivation and mentorship have been instrumental in empowering educators and shaping a new horizon in the field of education. His dedication to fostering innovative practices and inspiring change serves as a beacon for all who strive to enhance the learning experience. May his commitment to excellence continue to illuminate the path for educators and learners alike.

Contents

Foreword

Education goes beyond simply imparting knowledge; it forms the bedrock on which individuals construct their lives, communities, and societies. In our rapidly changing world, educators carry a profound responsibility—not only to share knowledge but also to shape a generation capable of confronting complex, global issues. As digital transformation accelerates, teaching methods evolve, and the balance between traditional wisdom and modern approaches becomes essential, the role of the educator has never been more crucial. Empowering Educators: New Horizons in Education is crafted with this vision in mind, offering guidance and inspiration for educators to embrace change, nurture creativity, and promote holistic growth.

The work before you is a comprehensive and thoughtful exploration of what it means to be an educator in the 21st century. As our world becomes increasingly interconnected, the boundaries between disciplines, cultures, and generations are shifting, and so must our approach to education. This book recognizes the need for an educational framework that empowers educators to adapt and thrive within this ever-changing landscape, offering them the tools and insights needed to cultivate resilient, innovative, and compassionate learners.

This book is dedicated to the incredible influence of Mr. Utsav Rahul Tiwari, Chief Operating Officer, whose commitment to empowering educators has been instrumental in shaping the vision of this work. His mentorship and support underscore a profound dedication to transforming education, not only by inspiring teachers but also by fostering a new horizon in educational thought and practice. His guidance has been invaluable in bringing forth this work, which aims to serve as both a roadmap and a source of inspiration for educators worldwide.

Empowering Minds: New Horizons in Education traverses the contemporary landscape of education, addressing key concepts such as active learning, collaborative methodologies, technology integration, and the inclusion of indigenous knowledge systems. It reimagines the role of the teacher from merely a purveyor of knowledge to a catalyst for growth, capable of nurturing curiosity, critical thinking, and ethical responsibility in their students. The book challenges educators to view teaching not as a task but as an opportunity to shape futures, instill values, and build the foundation for lifelong learning.

With each chapter, this book unfolds practical strategies, innovative frameworks, and insightful reflections that are relevant to today's educational challenges. Whether you are a seasoned educator or an emerging teacher, this work invites you to reflect, re-evaluate, and rejuvenate your approach to teaching. By embracing these new horizons in education, we can look forward to creating not only more capable students but also a more empathetic, resilient, and interconnected world.

As you read through the pages of Empowering Minds: New Horizons in Education, may you be inspired to see beyond traditional paradigms and embrace a transformative vision for education. I believe this book will serve as a valuable resource for those seeking to redefine and reimagine their role as educators, equipping them with the wisdom and tools to meet the demands of our times with optimism, innovation, and courage.

Dr. (D.Litt.) Frances Ketan Vaidya

Preface

In an age of unprecedented change, the role of education is being redefined to meet the demands of a fast-paced, interconnected world. Empowering Minds: New Horizons in Educationemerges from a deep recognition of the profound impact educators have on not only imparting knowledge but also shaping a generation equipped to tackle complex, global challenges. Education today is no longer limited to classrooms and textbooks; it is a lifelong journey, guiding individuals to construct meaningful lives, build stronger communities, and contribute to a resilient, just society.

This book reflects an understanding that educators are not simply knowledge-bearers but also catalysts for transformation. As digital advancements reshape how we learn and interact, and as teaching methodologies evolve, educators find themselves at the intersection of tradition and innovation. Balancing these elements is crucial, as both have valuable roles to play in fostering an environment where students can think critically, adapt creatively, and embrace values that transcend cultural and generational boundaries. Educators today are called upon to inspire curiosity, build resilience, and champion holistic development, nurturing skills that will empower learners to face future challenges with confidence and compassion.

Empowering Minds: New Horizons in Education is both a guide and a call to action, providing educators with insights, strategies, and perspectives to embrace new horizons in education. Each chapter explores the essential elements that define effective and transformative education today—from active learning and technology integration to collaborative approaches and the inclusion of indigenous knowledge systems. This book seeks to empower educators with the tools they need to inspire a new generation, ensuring that their teaching fosters not only intellectual growth but also ethical responsibility and global citizenship.

This work is dedicated to all educators who see beyond traditional paradigms, who innovate in the face of adversity, and who are committed to creating a more inclusive, empathetic, and sustainable future. It is also inspired by the vision and guidance of Mr. Utsav Rahul Tiwari, whose mentorship has been instrumental in bringing this work to life. His dedication to empowering educators has underscored the importance of continually seeking new horizons, fostering a culture of learning and growth that extends far beyond the classroom.

I invite you, as a reader and an educator, to delve into these pages with an open mind and a sense of purpose. May this book serve as a resource for not only navigating the challenges of today but also envisioning the possibilities of tomorrow, encouraging you to empower your students to build a brighter, more interconnected world.

Dr.(D.Litt.) Frances Ketan Vaidya

Acknowledgements

Empowering Minds: New Horizons in Education has been a journey of inspiration and collaboration, and I am deeply grateful to everyone who contributed to its realization.

My heartfelt thanks go to the entire management of Rahul Education, whose vision and dedication to advancing the teaching profession provided the foundation for this work. Their commitment to empowering educators and fostering an environment of innovation and excellence has been a driving force behind this book.

I am also immensely thankful to the remarkable staff of Rahul College of Education, , Vice Principal Sanjana Mishra, Assistant Professors Yigal Banker, Joyce Britto, Sarita Vishwakarma, Jaya Pathak, Bhagyashree Vywahare, and Mr. Rajesh Singh, whose dedication and passion in the teaching-learning process have consistently enriched the educational experience of our students. Their tireless efforts in developing innovative strategies, supporting students, and nurturing a culture of lifelong learning have been instrumental in making this work possible.

To the students of Rahul College of Education, I extend my deepest gratitude. Your curiosity, resilience, and commitment to learning inspire me every day. This book is dedicated to you, the future educators, who will carry forward the mission of empowering the next generation and shaping a better, more inclusive world.

Finally, I am grateful to everyone who has supported this endeavor in ways both big and small. This book is a testament to the collaborative spirit of those who believe in the transformative power of education, and I hope it serves as a source of inspiration and guidance for all who are committed to the noble path of teaching.

Dr.(D.Litt.) Frances Ketan Vaidya

Prologue

As we stand on the threshold of an era defined by rapid change and unprecedented challenges, the role of the educator has never been more vital or transformative. Education today is not merely about disseminating facts and figures; it is about instilling purpose, nurturing resilience, and preparing learners to engage thoughtfully with a world that is both complex and interconnected. The journey to empower educators to rise to this challenge forms the heart of Empowering Educators: New Horizons in Education.

Throughout history, education has been the key to unlocking human potential and fostering societal progress. But in today's dynamic environment, educators face demands that call for more than traditional methods. They are asked to be visionaries who balance the wisdom of the past with the tools of the future, merging conventional practices with groundbreaking technologies and diverse perspectives. This book recognizes the profound influence that empowered educators wield—not only in their classrooms but in shaping the worldviews, ethical foundations, and critical thinking skills of the next generation.

In a time where information is abundant but wisdom can be elusive, the educator's role expands to be one of guidance, mentorship, and inspiration. Educators today are pioneers of change, agents who spark curiosity, and champions of values that will carry their students forward. They bridge the divide between local and global, tradition and innovation, as they help students develop the knowledge, skills, and empathy necessary to thrive in a diverse, ever-evolving world.

Empowering Minds: New Horizons in Education is dedicated to this journey. It is crafted for educators who understand that teaching is more than a profession—it is a mission. This book provides practical strategies and fresh insights to help teachers embrace new approaches, explore innovative methodologies, and reflect on their impact. With each chapter, educators are invited to rediscover their power to influence lives, transform communities, and create a future that values learning, compassion, and sustainability.

As you embark on this journey through the pages of Empowering Minds: New Horizons in Education, may you feel inspired to approach your role with renewed vision and purpose. In doing so, you join a collective movement of educators worldwide who are shaping a brighter, more inclusive tomorrow.

Dr. (D.Litt.) Frances Ketan Vaidya

Dr. Frances Ketan Vaidya,Principal, Rahul College of Education

"Education is not the filling of a pail, but the lighting of a fire." – William Butler Yeats

In today's world, where knowledge is abundant yet wisdom sometimes hard to find, the role of an educator is both a privilege and a responsibility. Education, at its core, is about kindling curiosity, sparking a passion for discovery, and nurturing values that transcend generations. This book, '**Empowering Minds: New Horizons in Education"**, was born out of a deep belief that teaching is not merely a profession—it is a mission to inspire, guide, and uplift.

My hope is that this book will serve as a resource for teachers who wish to approach their work with renewed vision and purpose, embracing both innovation and the wisdom of the past. Each page invites you to explore new ideas, challenge conventions, and reflect on your own path as an educator. I am honored to share this journey with you and grateful to everyone who contributed to making this work possible.

As you read through these chapters, I encourage you to embrace your role not just as a teacher but as a catalyst for positive change. Together, we can shape a brighter future, one that is grounded in empathy, resilience, and a commitment to lifelong learning.

Thank you for joining me on this path of empowerment and growth.

Dr. (D.Litt.) Frances Ketan Vaidya

I

Active Learning: Fostering Engagement and Critical Thinking

"Tell me and I forget, teach me and I may remember, involve me and I learn."— *Benjamin Franklin*

In today's rapidly evolving educational landscape, traditional teaching methods are increasingly being replaced by approaches that engage students more deeply in their learning journey. At Rahul College of Education, the emphasis on **active learning** is transforming classrooms into dynamic spaces where students are not just passive recipients of information but active participants in constructing their own knowledge. Active learning shifts the focus from teacher-centred lectures to student-centred experiences, making learning interactive, collaborative, and reflective.

Active learning is a teaching approach that involves students in activities such as reading, writing, discussing, problem-solving, and critical thinking. It contrasts with passive learning, where students primarily listen to lectures or read content without much interaction. The goal of active learning is to enhance understanding, improve retention, and foster higher-order thinking skills like analysis, synthesis, and evaluation.

Active learning strategies at Rahul College of Education are embedded into the curriculum, helping future educators become adept at engaging their own students in meaningful learning experiences. By modelling these strategies, Rahul College of Education ensures that its student-teachers are well-prepared to bring innovative practices into their classrooms.

Collaborative learning is a cornerstone of the active learning approach at Rahul College of Education. In a typical classroom, students are grouped into teams to tackle complex problems, share insights, and co-create solutions. This method promotes peer learning, enhances communication skills, and fosters a sense of community. For example, during a unit on curriculum development, student-teachers work in groups to design lesson plans that incorporate both modern and traditional educational techniques. This collaboration allows them to pool their knowledge, critically analyze different approaches, and come up with innovative solutions. Group work helps in developing skills like leadership, team-building, and negotiation, which are essential for educators.

The **flipped classroo**m is another active learning strategy embraced at Rahul College of Education.

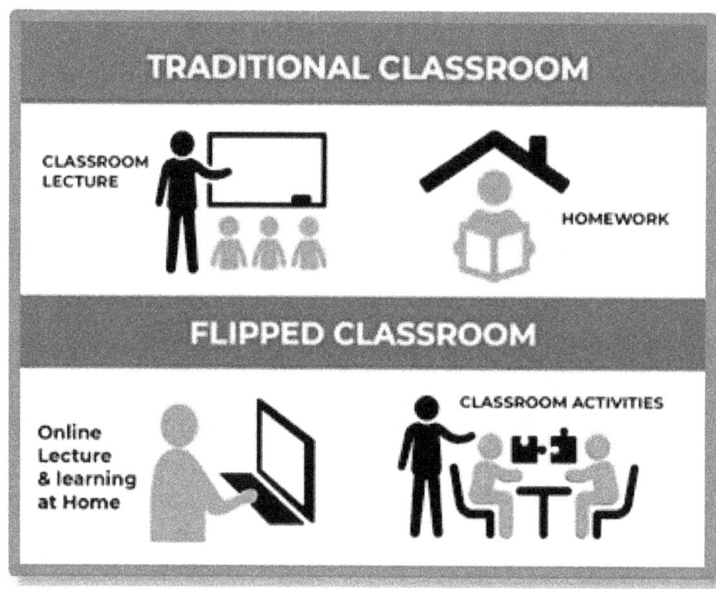

TRADITIONAL VERSUS FLIPPED CLASSROOM

In this model, traditional lectures are delivered through pre- recorded videos or readings that students complete outside of class. Classroom time is then used for discussions, group activities, and problem-solving.This approach allows for more interactive and personalized learning during class. Students come prepared with foundational knowledge, which enables them to engage more deeply with the material. For instance, in a course on educational psychology, student-teachers might watch a video on cognitive development theories before class and then engage in activities that apply these theories to real-life teaching scenarios.

Case-based learning is frequently used at Rahul College of Education to develop critical thinking and problem-solving skills. In this method, students are presented with real-life cases related to education, and they are tasked with analyzing the situations, identifying key issues, and proposing practical solutions.

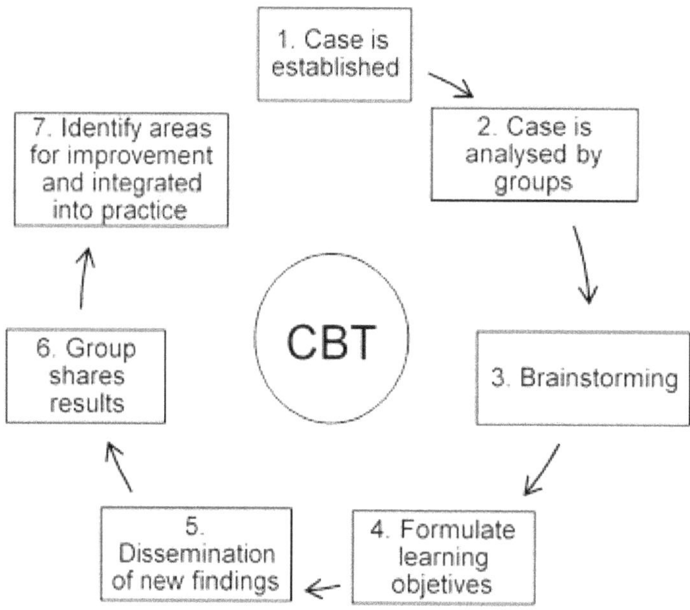

CASE BASED TEACHING PROCESS

For instance, a class on classroom management may use a case where a teacher is struggling to maintain discipline in a diverse classroom. Students work in groups to identify potential causes of the problem and suggest evidence-based strategies to address it. This approach helps student-teachers apply theoretical knowledge to practical situations, preparing them for challenges they might face in their teaching careers.

Project-based learning is a long-term, hands-on approach where students investigate and respond to complex questions or challenges.

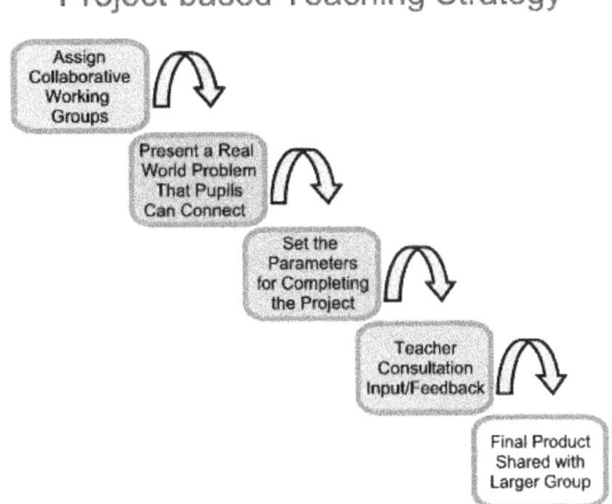

At Rahul College of Education, Project Based Teaching strategy is integrated into courses across disciplines, allowing students to work on projects that are relevant to their future roles as educators. In one notable project, student-teachers at Rahul College of Education develop a comprehensive school improvement plan based on data from local schools. They analyze student performance, teacher effectiveness, and community engagement, and propose strategies for enhancing the quality of education. This type of active learning project not only sharpens research and analytical skills but also instils a sense of responsibility and leadership.

Peer teaching is a powerful active learning strategy where students teach one another under the supervision of faculty. At Rahul College of Education, peer teaching is used to reinforce concepts and build confidence in student-teachers. It allows students to learn from multiple perspectives and develop their own teaching styles.For example, in a methodology class, student-teachers might take turns teaching mini-lessons on various instructional strategies. Their peers provide feedback, and faculty members offer guidance, helping to refine their teaching practices. This process encourages reflection, critical thinking, and continuous improvement.

Simulations and role-playing activities are widely used at Rahul College of Education to provide immersive learning experiences. These activities place students in realistic scenarios where they must apply their knowledge and skills in a controlled environment. For instance, in a course on conflict resolution, student-teachers might role-play as teachers, students, and parents during a simulated parent-teacher meeting. They practice resolving conflicts, communicating effectively, and managing difficult situations. This type of experiential learning helps student-teachers gain practical experience in a risk-free setting.

Reflection is an integral part of active learning at Rahul College of Education. Student-teachers are encouraged to reflect on their learning experiences, identify areas for improvement, and develop strategies for future growth. Reflective journals, portfolios, and group discussions are common tools used to facilitate reflection.For example, after completing a teaching practicum, students write reflective essays on their experiences in the classroom. They assess their strengths and weaknesses, consider feedback from mentors, and set goals for their continued professional development. This process helps future educators become more self-aware and committed to lifelong learning. At Rahul College of Education **formative assessments** are used throughout the learning process to provide immediate feedback to students. Rather than relying solely on summative assessments like final exams, formative assessments help student-teachers gauge their progress and make adjustments to their learning strategies.

Techniques such as quick quizzes, one-minute papers, and peer assessments are commonly used. These methods help students identify gaps in their understanding and receive constructive feedback in real-time. This ongoing assessment encourages active engagement with the Technology plays a crucial role in facilitating active learning at Rahul College of Education. Interactive platforms, educational apps, and digital tools are integrated into the learning process to make education more engaging and accessible. Tools like Google Classroom, Kahoot, and Padlet are frequently used to encourage collaboration, creativity, and active participation. In a course on educational technology, for instance, student-teachers might design interactive lessons using digital tools that they will eventually use in their own classrooms. This not only familiarizes them with technology but also empowers them to use these tools to enhance their future students' learning experiences.

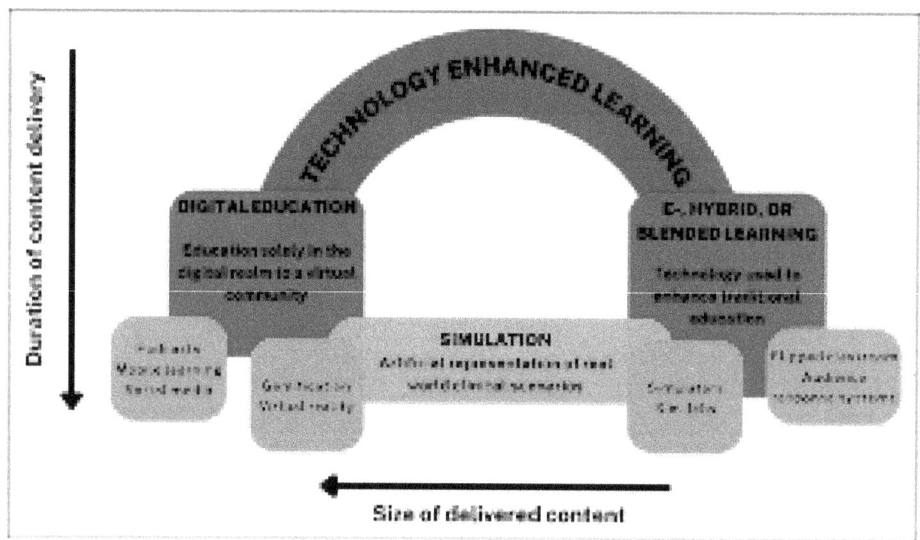

The Impact of Active Learning on student -teachers

The integration of active learning at Rahul College of Education has led to several positive outcomes for both students and faculty. Students are more motivated to participate in class, as they are actively involved in discussions, projects, and hands-on activities. The interactive nature of active learning makes education more engaging and enjoyable.Active learning encourages students to analyze, synthesize, and material and promotes a growth mindset. evaluate information rather than simply memorizing facts. This leads to deeper understanding and the ability to apply knowledge in real-world situations.

Through group work, peer teaching, and collaborative projects, students develop essential teamwork and communication skills that are vital for their future careers as educators. By engaging in case studies, simulations, and project-based learning, student-teachers are better prepared to handle the complexities of the modern classroom. They gain practical experience and develop problem-solving skills that are crucial for effective teaching.

The reflective nature of active learning fosters a growth mindset, encouraging students to continuously seek knowledge and improve their teaching practices throughout their careers.

Conclusion

At Rahul College of Education, active learning is not just a pedagogical approach but a philosophy that permeates the entire educational experience. By placing students at the center of their learning journey, the college equips future educators with the skills, knowledge, and confidence they need to succeed in the 21st-century classroom. Active learning prepares students not just to pass exams but to become innovative, reflective, and compassionate teachers who can inspire the next generation of learners.

References:

- Bonwell, C.C., & Eison, J.A. (1991). *Active Learning: Creating Excitement in the Classroom.* ASHE-ERIC Higher Education Report No. 1. George Washington University.
- Prince, M. (2004). "Does active learning work? A review of the research." *Journal of Engineering Education*, 93(3), 22
- Barkley, E.F., Major, C.H., & Cross, K.P. (2014). *Collaborative Learning Techniques: A Handbook for College Faculty.*

II

Personalized Learning: Crafting Tailored Educational Journeys

"Every student can learn, just not on the same day or in the same way."— *George Evans*

In an era of rapid technological advancements and evolving pedagogical practices, the one- Size-fits-all model of education is becoming obsolete. Instead, educational institutions are increasingly adopting more flexible and tailored approaches to teaching and learning. Rahul College of Education, a pioneering institution in teacher training, is at the forefront of this movement with its focus on personalized learning. By embracing personalized learning, the college is ensuring that each student-teacher embarks on a unique educational journey tailored to their individual needs, learning styles, and future aspirations. Personalized learning is an instructional approach that aims to customize learning experiences to meet the diverse needs of individual students. It acknowledges that students have different strengths, weaknesses, interests, and learning paces. By providing a more flexible learning environment, personalized learning empowers students to take control of their education, working towards mastery of skills and concepts at their own pace. At Rahul College of Education, personalized learning is not just a buzzword—it is a core element of the institution's teaching philosophy. The college integrates a variety of tools and strategies to ensure that student-teachers are receiving an education that is relevant, engaging, and suited to their personal and professional goals.

PERSONALIZED LEARNING AT RAHUL COLLEGE OF EDUCATION

One of the most critical components of personalized learning at Rahul College of Education is the development of **Individual Learning Plans (ILPs)**. Upon enrolment, each student-teacher works closely with academic advisors and faculty to develop an ILP that maps out their learning objectives, career goals, and areas of focus. The ILP is a dynamic document that evolves over time, allowing for adjustments based on the student-teacher's progress, interests, and emerging needs. For example, a student-teacher with a keen interest in educational technology might have an ILP that emphasizes courses, workshops, and projects related to integrating technology into the classroom. Another student-teacher who is passionate about special education might focus on gaining expertise in inclusive teaching practices and developing customized teaching materials for diverse learners. At Rahul College of Education, the rigid structure of traditional education is replaced with a more flexible approach to learning. In a personalized learning environment, student-teachers are encouraged to progress at their own pace, ensuring that they fully understand and master a concept before moving on to the next one. This approach is particularly beneficial for future educators, as it models a student-centered method of teaching that they can later implement in their own classrooms. Rather than being constrained by a semester-based schedule, students can take additional time if they need it or move ahead more quickly if they demonstrate mastery of a topic. This flexibility ensures that students are not left behind or forced to rush through material. It also promotes a deeper understanding of content, as students can revisit challenging topics as needed without the pressure of fixed deadlines.

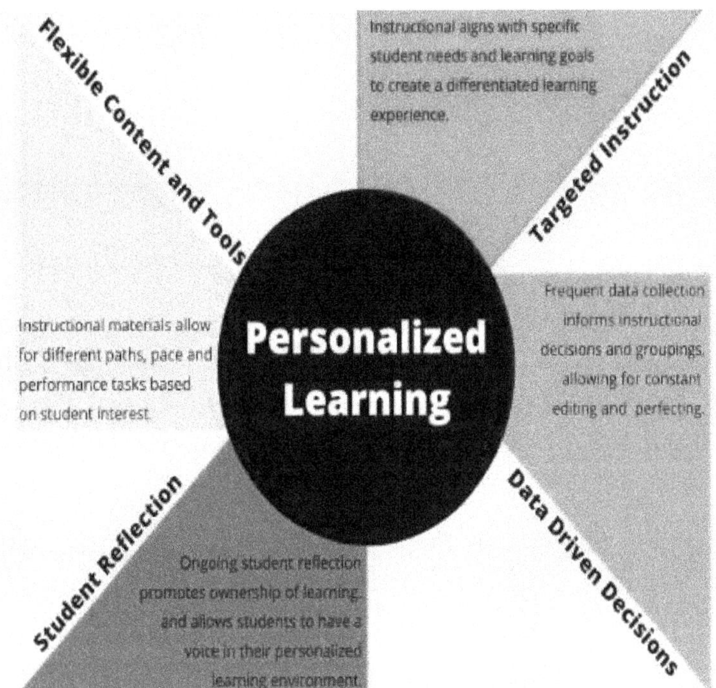

PERSONALIZED LEARNING PROCESS

Personalized learning at Rahul College of Education allows student-teachers to choose from a variety of learning pathways based on their interests and career goals. This choice is reflected in both the curriculum and the extracurricular opportunities offered at the college. For instance, student-teachers can choose to specialize in areas such as early childhood education, secondary education, special education, or educational leadership.Moreover, within courses, student-teachers are often given the freedom to choose how they demonstrate their understanding of the material. For example, in a course on educational psychology, students might have the option to write a research paper, develop a presentation, or create a classroom activity that applies psychological theories to teaching. This level of choice not only empowers student-teachers but also fosters creativity and engagement in their learning.

Technology plays a significant role in facilitating personalized learning at Rahul College of Education. The college has integrated **adaptive learning technologies** that tailor educational content based on the performance and learning style of each student. These platforms use algorithms to analyze student data, such as quiz results or interaction patterns, and adjust the difficulty level or type of content accordingly.For example, if a student-teacher is struggling with a particular concept in a course on teaching methodologies, the adaptive learning platform might offer additional resources, such as videos, readings, or practice exercises, to help them grasp the material. Conversely, if a student demonstrates mastery of a topic, the system may present more advanced content or allow them to move on to the next unit. This technology ensures that each student is learning at the optimal level of difficulty for their abilities.

Personalized learning at Rahul College of Education is bolstered by a strong **mentorship** system. Each student-teacher is paired with a faculty mentor who provides guidance, support, and feedback throughout their academic journey. Mentors work closely with student-teachers to help them set realistic goals, overcome challenges, and stay on track with their learning plans.One-on-one support is also provided through regular check-ins with academic advisors, who help student-teachers reflect on their progress and adjust their ILPs as needed. This personalized attention ensures that students are not just passive participants in their education but are actively shaping their learning experience.

At Rahul College of Education, the use of **data-driven instruction** is an essential aspect of personalized learning. Faculty members and academic advisors use data from assessments, classroom interactions, and digital learning platforms to monitor student progress and identify areas where additional support is needed. This data-driven approach allows for timely interventions and adjustments to the curriculum to better meet the needs of each student.For example, if data indicates that a student-teacher is struggling with lesson planning, the faculty can provide additional resources, suggest supplementary workshops, or offer one-on- one coaching to help the student overcome this challenge. Data-driven insights help ensure that no student falls through the cracks and that each individual receives the support they need to succeed.

Personalized learning at Rahul College of Education often involves **interdisciplinary projects** that allow student-teachers to explore their interests in a hands-on, real-world context. These projects not only reinforce classroom learning but also give students the opportunity to pursue topics that are meaningful to them.For example, a student-teacher interested in environmental education might work on a project that integrates science, social studies, and environmental advocacy. They could design a curriculum for teaching sustainability in schools, develop lesson plans for various grade levels, and present their findings to a panel of educators and community leaders. This type of project- based learning allows student-teachers to apply their knowledge in a practical setting while pursuing their individual passions.

Rahul College of Education is committed to making personalized learning accessible to all students, including those with diverse learning needs. The college incorporates **inclusive education practices** that ensure that students with disabilities or learning challenges receive the support they need to succeed.For example, students with dyslexia or other learning differences may receive accommodations such as extended time on assignments, access to assistive technology, or individualized support from faculty. Personalized learning at Rahul College of Education is designed to be flexible enough to accommodate the unique needs of all students, ensuring that everyone has the opportunity to thrive.

Reflection is a key aspect of personalized learning at Rahul College of Education. Student-teachers are encouraged to engage in **reflective learning**, where they regularly assess their progress, identify areas for improvement, and set new goals. Reflective journals, self- assessments, and peer reviews are commonly used to help students develop self-awareness and a growth mindset.

This reflective process ensures that personalized learning is not static but evolves over time as students grow and develop. By encouraging continuous improvement, Rahul College of Education instills in its student-teachers the habits of lifelong learners who are committed to personal and professional growth.

The Impact of Personalized Learning on the Students

The personalized learning approach at Rahul College of Education has had a profound impact on student outcomes. Student-teachers are more engaged in their learning because they have a voice in shaping their educational journey. The freedom to choose learning pathways and pacing makes education more relevant and meaningful. By progressing at their own pace and focusing on mastery, student-teachers develop a deeper understanding of the material. This depth of knowledge better prepares them for their future roles as educators. Personalized learning empowers student-teachers by giving them control over their education. This empowerment fosters confidence, independence, and a strong sense of responsibility. Student- teachers at Rahul College of Education graduate with the skills and knowledge needed to implement personalized learning in their own classrooms. They are better equipped to meet the diverse needs of their future students and to create inclusive, engaging learning environments.

Conclusion

At Rahul College of Education, personalized learning is not just a method—it is a philosophy that recognizes and nurtures the unique potential of each student-teacher. By offering flexible, tailored educational experiences, the college ensures that its graduates are not only well- prepared for the challenges of modern teaching but are also lifelong learners who are capable of adapting to the ever-changing demands of education. Personalized learning at Rahul College of Education is transforming the future of education, one student-teacher at a time.

References

- Pane, J.F., Steiner, E.D., Baird, M.D., & Hamilton, L.S. (2017). *Continued Progress: Promising Evidence on Personalized Learning.* RAND Corporation.
- Bray, B., & McClaskey, K. (2014). *Personalized Learning: A Guide for Engaging Students with Voice and Choice.* Corwin.
- Wolf, M.A. (2010). *Innovate to Educate: System [Re]Design for Personalized Learning.* A Report by the Software & Information Industry Association.

III

Collaborative Learning: Fostering Teamwork and Cooperative Knowledge Construction

"**Alone we can do so little; together we can do so much.**"— ***Helen Keller***

In today's dynamic educational landscape, collaborative learning has emerged as a vital pedagogical approach. It not only enriches the learning experience but also prepares students for the collaborative environments they will encounter in their future careers. **Rahul College of Education**, an institution committed to training future educators, places a strong emphasis on collaborative learning as part of its teacher education program. This approach aligns with modern educational needs, fostering teamwork, communication, and shared problem-solving among student-teachers.

Collaborative learning at Rahul College of Education is woven into the curriculum through various strategies and learning models. The overarching goal is to ensure that student-teachers become well- equipped to work together, solve problems creatively, and apply their collective knowledge in practical, real-world educational settings.Collaborative learning is an instructional approach where students work together in small groups to explore a problem, complete a task, or achieve a common goal. It differs from traditional classroom settings in which individual work and competition are emphasized. Collaborative learning encourages the pooling of resources and ideas, promoting a shared responsibility for learning outcomes.

COLLABORATIVE LEARNING AT RAHUL COLLEGE OF EDUCATION

At Rahul College of Education, collaborative learning is designed not only to help student- teachers understand course content but also to develop critical professional skills such as communication, leadership, empathy, and conflict resolution. By learning how to work effectively in teams, student-teachers can better implement similar strategies in their future classrooms. One of the primary features of collaborative learning at Rahul College of Education is **group-based learning**, where student-teachers are organized into small groups to work on specific tasks. Whether in classroom discussions, assignments, or projects, student-teachers are expected to collaborate with their peers to complete tasks.For example, in a course on instructional strategies, student-teachers might be grouped together to develop lesson plans for different grade levels. Each group member takes responsibility for different aspects of the lesson, such as content delivery, student engagement, and assessment group is responsible for researching the topic,designing lesson plans, and developing assessments tailored to different grade levels. The final project is presented to the class, followed by a reflective discussion on the collaborative process and what they learned from working together. Through this process, student-teachers learn howto coordinate their efforts, share ideas, and come to a consensus on how best to meet educational objectives.

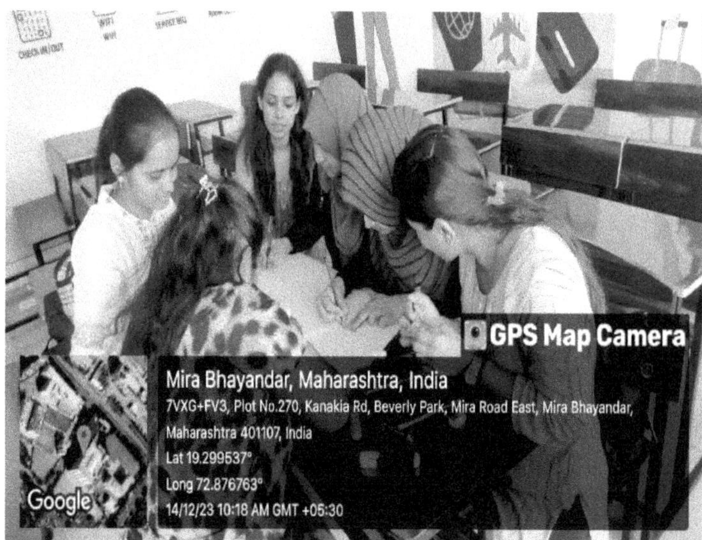

Group-Based Learning

At Rahul College of Education, **project-based learning** (PBL) plays a significant role in fostering collaboration. This method involves students working together on long-term projects that require in-depth research, planning, and execution. PBL not only promotes collaboration but also mirrors the type of teamwork required in real-life educational settings. For instance, student-teachers might be tasked with creating a comprehensive unit plan on an interdisciplinary theme, such as environmental sustainability or cultural diversity in education. Each group is responsible for researching the topic, designing lesson plans, and developing assessments tailored to different grade levels. The final project is presented to the class, followed by a reflective discussion on the collaborative process and what they learned from working together.

Peer teaching is another key element of collaborative learning at Rahul College of Education. In this approach, student-teachers are given the opportunity to teach their peers as part of their learning process. This method not only reinforces their own understanding of the material but also fosters a sense of shared responsibility for each other's learning.For example, in a classroom management course, student-teachers may take turns presenting case studies to their peers and leading discussions on how to handle various classroom situations. By teaching their peers, student-teachers deepen their own knowledge of the subject matter while practicing essential skills such as public speaking and classroom facilitation.

Collaborative problem-solving is a critical component of the learning process at Rahul College of Education. In this approach, student-teachers work together to solve complex problems, often using real-life case studies that reflect challenges faced by educators in schools today. These case studies allow student-teachers to apply theoretical knowledge to practical situations, developing both their problem-solving abilities and their collaborative skills.

For instance, a group of student-teachers might be presented with a case study where a fictional school is struggling with low student engagement. The group is tasked with analyzing the situation, identifying potential causes, and proposing strategies to improve student engagement. By working together to brainstorm solutions and share perspectives, the student-teachers gain a deeper understanding of the multifaceted nature of educational problems and the importance of collaboration in finding effective solutions. At Rahul College of Education of education, technology plays an important role in facilitating **collaborative learning**, especially in blended or online learning environments. Digital platforms such as Google Classroom, Microsoft Teams, and Padlet are used to enable student-teachers to collaborate remotely, share documents, and provide feedback on each other's work in real-time.For example, during a group assignment on educational policy analysis, student-teachers might use Google Docs to collaboratively write a report, with each member contributing research and editing the document simultaneously.

Tools like Trello can help groups organize tasks, assign responsibilities, and track progress. This use of technology not only supports collaboration but also prepares student-teachers to use similar tools in their own future classrooms to facilitate student teamwork.

In collaborative learning, the role of the faculty shifts from being a sole provider of knowledge to a **facilitator of learning**. At Rahul College of Education, faculty members guide the collaborative learning process by providing clear objectives, structuring activities, and offering feedback to ensure that group interactions are productive and focused.Faculty members at Rahul College of Education often set specific roles within groups, such as discussion leader, note-taker, or project manager, to ensure that each group member contributes to the task at hand. For example, in a collaborative research project on inclusive education, the instructor might assign each group member a role that aligns with their strengths while also encouraging them to take responsibility for the group's overall success.Collaborative learning at Rahul College of Education also extends to the assessment process. Student-teachers often participate in **collaborative assessments**, where they are evaluated as a group based on their collective work. This approach emphasizes the importance of shared responsibility and teamwork in achieving learning outcomes.

In some cases, peer feedback is also an essential part of the assessment process. For example, after completing a group project, student-teachers might be asked to evaluate each other's contributions and reflect on how effectively the group worked together. This feedback process helps students develop self-awareness, recognize the value of collaboration, and identify areas for improvement.Rahul College of Education encourages **interdisciplinary collaboration**, where student-teachers from different subject areas work together to create cross-disciplinary lesson plans. For example, a group might combine mathematics and environmental science to develop a unit on "Math in Nature," where students learn geometry concepts through the study of natural patterns such as the Fibonacci sequence in plants. In courses on lesson planning and curriculum design, student- teachers participate in **peer review workshops**. They present their lesson plans to their peers for feedback, encouraging a culture of open communication and constructive criticism. The feedback process allows student-teachers to reflect on their teaching strategies and improve their work based on input from their colleagues.

Concept mapping is a collaborative tool used at Rahul College of Education to help student-teachers visualize and organize complex information. In a course on educational psychology, for example, groups of student-teachers might create a concept map to illustrate how various psychological theories (e.g., behaviorism, constructivism) are connected and applied in classroom settings. Working together to construct the map promotes deep engagement with the material and helps students make connections between concepts.

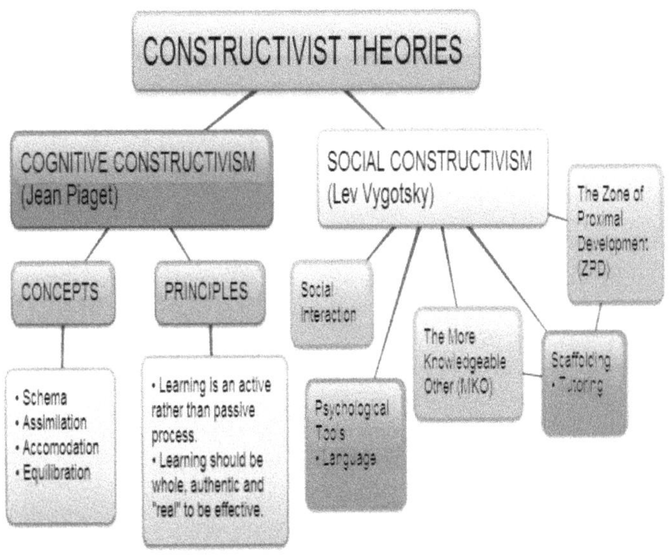

CONCEPT MAPPING

The Benefits of Collaborative Learning

By working together, student-teachers learn to analyze problems from multiple perspectives and develop critical thinking skills. Collaborative learning fosters communication, negotiation, and conflict resolution skills, all of which are essential for effective teaching. Collaborative projects mirror the teamwork required in schools, preparing student-teachers to work with colleagues, parents, and administrators in their future roles. Working in groups increases student engagement by making learning more interactive and participatory. Collaborative learning fosters a sense of community and support among student-teachers, helping them build strong professional networks.

Conclusion

Collaborative learning at Rahul College of Education is a cornerstone of the institution's approach to teacher training. By encouraging student-teachers to work together on projects, solve problems collaboratively, and engage in peer teaching, the college ensures that its graduates are not only knowledgeable in their subject areas but also equipped with the interpersonal and professional skills necessary for success in the modern educational landscape. Collaborative learning prepares future educators to create dynamic, interactive, and inclusive learning environments where students work together to achieve shared goals.

References

- Johnson, D.W., Johnson, R.T., & Smith, K.A. (1998). *Cooperative Learning Returns to College:What Evidence Is There That It Works?* Change: The Magazine of Higher Learning, 30(4), 26-35.
- Barkley, E.F., Major, C.H., & Cross, K.P. (2014). *Collaborative Learning Techniques: A Handbook for College Faculty.* Jossey-Bass.
- Slavin, R.E. (1996). *Research on cooperative learning and achievement: What we know, what we need to know.* Contemporary Educational Psychology, 21(1), 43-69.

IV

Learning through Films: Enhancing Teacher Education through Audio Visual Media

"Film is the most powerful agent of social change. It is also a powerful educational tool, turning passive viewers into active learners."— *David Puttnam*

In the rapidly evolving educational landscape, innovative teaching methods are crucial for preparing future educators to engage and inspire their students. **Learning through films** is one such method that has gained traction as an effective pedagogical tool. At **Rahul College of Education**, the incorporation of films into the curriculum plays a significant role in enhancing the learning experience for student-teachers. By leveraging the power of visual storytelling, films provide a dynamic and engaging medium for exploring complex concepts, promoting critical thinking, and developing empathy.

The Role of Films in Education

Films have long been recognized as powerful educational tools due to their ability to convey ideas, emotions, and narratives in a compelling and accessible way . Using films in the education of student-teachers can serve as a powerful tool to enhance learning, particularly in areas such as theoretical understanding, cultural sensitivity, critical thinking, and emotional engagement. Films have the unique ability to transform abstract ideas into concrete, visually engaging experiences. For student-teachers, who often deal with pedagogical theories and psychological frameworks, films can serve as examples of how these concepts play out in real-world or fictionalized classroom settings. For example, films about education can depict scenarios related to classroom management, teaching methods, or child development theories in action. Seeing these concepts applied in context makes it easier for student-teachers to grasp and retain information, as well as to apply these ideas in their own teaching practice. This method also helps accommodate visual learners who benefit from seeing ideas represented visually.

One of the critical roles of educators is to foster an inclusive classroom environment that respects and acknowledges cultural diversity. Films provide an immersive experience into different cultures, beliefs, and traditions, which can help student-teachers become more aware of the socio-cultural backgrounds of their future students. By watching films that portray the experiences of people from various cultural groups, student-teachers can develop empathy and an understanding of the different perspectives their students may bring into the classroom. This awareness can be particularly useful when addressing topics such as multicultural education, social justice, and equity in education, helping future teachers to design more inclusive lesson plans and classroom strategies.

Films often present complex social, ethical, and pedagogical issues that challenge viewers to think deeply about the implications of their actions and decisions. For student-teachers, films can serve as case studies that require them to analyze situations, identify underlying issues, and reflect on possible solutions. For example, films that portray issues of inequality, bullying, or moral dilemmas in education can stimulate classroom discussions where student-teachers debate solutions, challenge biases, and critically examine their own beliefs. This type of engagement helps develop problem-solving skills, critical thinking, and the ability to reflect on one's professional values and teaching philosophy.

The emotional impact of films is well-documented, and this can be harnessed in the educational context to foster deeper connections with learning material. For student-teachers, films can evoke emotions that mirror the challenges and triumphs educators face in their daily work. Experiencing these emotions through the narratives in films can help future teachers cultivate empathy—an essential trait for anyone working with students. Whether it's a film that deals with the struggles of marginalized students or one that showcases the power of resilience and perseverance, emotional engagement helps student-teachers relate to their students on a human level. Moreover, it can motivate them to adopt more compassionate and supportive teaching practices.

At Rahul College of Education, films are integrated into various courses and activities to enhance the learning experience. These films range from documentaries to educational dramas, and each is selected based on its relevance to the curriculum and its potential to foster meaningful learning outcomes.One of the most effective uses of films at Rahul College of Education is as **case studies** that depict real-life educational challenges. Student-teachers watch films that portray different classroom scenarios, teaching strategies, and the challenges faced by educators. These films provide valuable insights into issues such as classroom management, student engagement, and inclusive education.For example, the film *"Stand and Deliver"* (1988) is frequently used in courses on instructional strategies. The film tells the story of a high school math teacher who uses unconventional teaching methods to inspire his underprivileged students to excel. After watching the film, student-teachers engage in discussions about the importance of teacher-student relationships, differentiated instruction, and overcoming barriers to learning. The film serves as a case study for exploring the role of perseverance and innovation in education. Similarly, *"Taare Zameen*

Par" (2007), a Bollywood film that highlights the struggles of a child with dyslexia, is used in courses on special education and inclusive teaching. The film provides a platform for student- teachers to discuss learning disabilities, the importance of individualized instruction, and the need for compassionate and empathetic teaching practices.

STUDENT-TEACHERS LEARNING THROUGH FILMS

Documentaries are also a key part of the learning process at Rahul College of Education. They provide factual, real-world perspectives on issues that impact education and society. Documentaries like ***"Waiting for Superman"*** (2010), which examines the challenges facing the American public education system, are used to spark discussions about global educational reform, inequality, and the role of teachers in shaping educational policy.By watching documentaries, student-teachers are exposed to diverse viewpoints on social issues such as poverty, gender inequality, and access to education. This helps them develop a broader understanding of the societal contexts in which education takes place, preparing them to be socially aware and responsive educators. Films that depict different teaching methods and philosophies allow student-teachers to critically analyze the effectiveness of various pedagogical approaches. For example, the film ***"Dead Poets Society"*** (1989) is often used in courses on teaching philosophy and classroom dynamics. The film showcases an unorthodox teacher who inspires his students to think independently and embrace creativity, challenging traditional methods of rote learning and conformity.

After watching such films, student-teachers engage in reflective discussions about how different teaching methods impact student engagement and learning outcomes. They are encouraged to compare the methods depicted in the films with the theories and strategies they have studied, critically evaluating the pros and cons of each approach.Films are particularly effective at fostering **empathy** and **cultural sensitivity**, which are essential qualities for future educators. By portraying characters from diverse backgrounds, films help student-teachers understand the challenges faced by students from different socio- economic, cultural, or linguistic backgrounds. films like ***"The Freedom Writers"*** (2007) depict the struggles of marginalized students and the power of education to change lives. Such films encourage student-teachers to reflect on their own biases, the importance of building inclusive classroom environments, and the role of educators in advocating for equity and justice in education.

Similarly, foreign-language films and films from different cultures, such as *"Like Stars on Earth"* (India), *"Children of Heaven"* (Iran), and *"The Class"* (France), provide valuable cultural insights that help student-teachers appreciate the diversity they will encounter in their own classrooms.

Learning Activities around Films

The use of films in the curriculum at Rahul College of Education is not limited to passive viewing. Films are integrated into **active learning** activities that encourage student-teachers to engage critically with the content. After watching a film, student-teachers participate in **group discussions** or debates, where they are encouraged to share their interpretations and perspectives. Faculty members guide these discussions by posing critical questions, prompting student-teachers to reflect on the pedagogical, ethical, and social issues raised in the film. After watching ***"Lean on Me"*** (1989), a film about a principal who takes drastic measures to reform a troubled inner-city school, student-teachers might debate the ethics of the principal's authoritarian approach. This activity helps student-teachers develop their critical thinking and communication skills while also deepening their understanding of leadership in education.

Reflective writing assignments are another important component of learning through films at Rahul College of Education. After watching a film, student-teachers are often asked to write reflections on how the film relates to their own experiences, values, and future roles as educators. These reflections encourage deep thinking and self-awareness, helping student-teachers internalize the lessons learned from the film.

For example, after watching *"The Great Debaters"* (2007), a film about an African-American debate team overcoming racial prejudice, student-teachers might write about the role of educators in addressing social justice issues and how they can foster a sense of empowerment in their own students.

In some courses, student-teachers are asked to work in groups to create **film-based projects** or presentations. They might analyze a specific film, create lesson plans based on the themes of the film, or even produce short educational films of their own. These projects promote collaboration, creativity, and the practical application of film-based learning in classroom settings.For example, a group of student-teachers might be tasked with creating a lesson plan for middle school students based on the themes of *"Akeelah and the Bee"* (2006), a film about a young girl's journey to compete in a national spelling bee. The lesson plan could focus on themes such as perseverance, self-confidence, and the power of mentorship.

Benefits of Learning through Films

Using films at Rahul College of Education in the educational process for student-teachers can significantly enrich their learning experience by promoting engagement, understanding, critical thinking, cultural awareness, and creativity. Films are inherently engaging because they combine visuals, sound, and narrative, making them a dynamic medium that easily captures attention. In an educational context, this engagement can be crucial for student-teachers who are often juggling theoretical coursework and practical training. When a film presents teaching strategies, classroom management scenarios, or even historical contexts of educational reform, student-teachers are more likely to become invested in the material. Films can break up the monotony of traditional lectures or reading assignments, making learning more enjoyable. Moreover, by incorporating real-life scenarios or dramatizations, films can foster emotional and intellectual involvement, leading to deeper retention of the subject matter.

Complex theories or concepts can often be difficult to understand in the abstract. Films bridge this gap by offering visual representations that can make these ideas more relatable and comprehensible. For example, educational theories such as Piaget's stages of cognitive development or Vygotsky's zone of proximal development can be illustrated through classroom settings in films, helping student-teachers see how these theories manifest in actual teaching practices. This process of seeing theoretical concepts in action allows student-teachers to build connections between what they learn in books and how it applies to their future teaching. Additionally, films often tell stories over a period of time, giving viewers a clearer sense of progression, growth, and how actions lead to outcomes in educational contexts.

Films naturally invite analysis and critique, as they present multi-layered stories, characters, and situations. For student-teachers, this is an opportunity to practice critical thinking, a skill that is essential in their profession. After watching a film, they can be asked to reflect on the motivations of characters, evaluate the ethical decisions made by teachers or administrators, and consider alternative approaches to handling various classroom situations. For example, if a film depicts a scenario involving a disruptive classroom, student-teachers can discuss how they would have handled the situation differently, considering their knowledge of classroom management techniques. This exercise encourages them to question assumptions, think creatively, and consider the consequences of different pedagogical choices.

Exposure to diverse perspectives is vital for student-teachers as they prepare to educate students from various cultural, social, and economic backgrounds. Films, especially those that explore different cultural or social settings, provide a window into the experiences of people who may be different from the student-teachers themselves. Watching films that explore themes of race, gender, disability, and socioeconomic status can help student-teachers develop a deeper sense of empathy and understanding for the students they will one day teach. This exposure helps them recognize their own biases and work towards creating an inclusive classroom environment where all students feel valued and respected. Empathy developed through films is a powerful tool for understanding the challenges that some students face both inside and outside the classroom.

Film-based projects can take learning beyond the passive act of watching. When student- teachers engage in creative assignments, such as creating their own short films or designing film-based lesson plans, they tap into their creativity and collaborative skills. These projects can be particularly useful in teaching methods courses, where student-teachers can reflect on how to incorporate multimedia resources into their own classrooms. Reflective writing assignments based on films can also encourage deeper self-reflection. For instance, after watching a film, student-teachers can write reflective essays that analyze the pedagogical strategies depicted and compare them to their own teaching philosophy. This process encourages student-teachers to think about how they can apply what they have learned from the film to their own professional practice, fostering a habit of continuous learning and self-improvement.

Conclusion

At Rahul College of Education, learning through films is more than just an entertaining diversion; it is a powerful pedagogical tool that enriches the learning experience of student- teachers. By incorporating films into the curriculum, the college fosters critical thinking, empathy, and a deep understanding of the complexities of education. Through the use of films, student-teachers at Rahul College of Education are better prepared to create engaging, inclusive, and culturally responsive classrooms, ultimately becoming more effective and compassionate educators.

References:

- Johnson, D.W., Johnson, R.T., & Smith, K.A. (1998). *Cooperative Learning Returns to College:What Evidence Is There That It Works?* Change: The Magazine of Higher Learning, 30(4), 26- 35.
- Barkley, E.F., Major, C.H., & Cross, K.P. (2014). *Collaborative Learning Techniques: A Handbook for College Faculty.* Jossey-Bass.
- Slavin, R.E. (1996). *Research on cooperative learning and achievement: What we know, what we need to know.* Contemporary Educational Psychology, 21(1), 43-69.

V

Constructivism Learning: Building Knowledge through Active Engagement

"Knowledge is not a commodity to be consumed; it is a construct to be created through active engagement and collaboration."— Jean Piaget

Constructivism is a widely recognized educational theory that emphasizes the learner's active role in constructing knowledge rather than passively receiving information. It focuses on learners making sense of the world through experiences, interactions, and reflections. At **Rahul College of Education**, constructivism serves as a cornerstone of the teaching philosophy, shaping how future educators are trained to approach learning and teaching in modern classrooms. Rahul College of Education embraces constructivism as a powerful framework that fosters critical thinking, problem-solving, and deep engagement with content. Student-teachers are encouraged to actively participate in their own learning process, making sense of educational theories and practices through exploration, reflection, and co llaboration.

Constructivism is based on the idea that knowledge is actively constructed by the learner rather than passively absorbed. Learners bring their prior experiences, beliefs, and knowledge to new learning situations, and they build upon this foundation by interacting with new information. In this way, learning is viewed as a personal and contextual process, where understanding is constructed through inquiry, exploration, and problem-solving. It is a learning theory that emphasizes the active role of learners in building their own understanding, with the teacher acting as a facilitator rather than a provider of knowledge.

In constructivist learning, students are not passive recipients of information. Instead, they are actively engaged in the learning process through exploration, questioning, and experimentation. This principle emphasizes that learning happens through doing rather than merely listening or memorizing. For example, in a classroom setting, a teacher might encourage students to solve a problem, conduct experiments, or engage in hands-on projects that require them to apply what they are learning. This approach fosters deeper understanding, as students construct their own knowledge through experience, reflection, and interaction with the material. Active learning encourages critical thinking and helps students develop the skills to become independent learners.

A foundational principle of constructivism is that learners build new knowledge based on what they already know. This concept, often referred to as "scaffolding," suggests that learning is an additive process, where new ideas are connected to prior experiences or knowledge. When learners can relate new information to existing knowledge, they are more likely to understand and retain the new concepts. For example, in teaching a complex concept like fractions, a teacher might first relate the concept to something familiar, like dividing a pizza, before moving on to more abstract representations. Recognizing and activating students' prior knowledge helps teachers tailor instruction to the learners' cognitive framework, making new learning more accessible and meaningful.

Constructivist theory emphasizes the role of social interaction in learning. Learners do not construct knowledge in isolation; they engage in dialogue, collaboration, and discussion with their peers and instructors. Through these interactions, learners can challenge, refine, and expand their understanding. Collaborative learning activities, such as group projects, discussions, and peer feedback, allow students to share diverse perspectives and build on each other's ideas. This exchange of ideas helps deepen understanding and encourages students to think critically about their own assumptions. Social interaction also mirrors the way knowledge is constructed in the real world, where collaboration and communication are key to solving complex problems.

In constructivism, learning is seen as inherently tied to the context in which it occurs. Knowledge is not abstract or decontextualized; rather, it is constructed within specific, relevant, and meaningful contexts. This principle underscores the importance of real-world applications and experiential learning. For example, instead of teaching mathematical formulas in isolation, a constructivist approach would integrate these formulas into practical, everyday scenarios— such as measuring materials for a building project or calculating expenses for a budget. When students see how their learning applies to the world around them, they are more motivated and engaged. This also fosters deeper comprehension, as students understand not just the "what" but also the "why" behind the knowledge they are acquiring. Reflection is a critical component of deep learning in constructivism. It involves students thinking about their experiences, understanding how they arrived at certain conclusions, and considering how they can apply this learning in new contexts. Reflection allows learners to connect new knowledge with existing knowledge, identify areas of confusion, and develop strategies for future learning. This could be facilitated through activities such as journaling,self-assessments, or classroom discussions where students explain their thought processes and learning experiences. Reflection helps consolidate learning and encourages a metacognitive approach, where students not only engage with the material but also think about how they are learning. This awareness fosters lifelong learning and continuous improvement.

At Rahul College of Education, these principles are embedded in the curriculum and pedagogy, allowing student-teachers to experience constructivist learning first hand and to apply it in their future teaching careers.The educators emphasizes **active learning environments** where student-teachers are not passive recipients of information, but rather, are engaged in meaningful tasks that require them to actively participate, question, and explore. Classrooms are designed to facilitate discussion, interaction, and collaboration, allowing student-teachers to engage with content deeply and critically. For example, in a course on child psychology, instead of merely listening to lectures about developmental stages, student-teachers are asked to observe children in different age groups, analyze their behavior, and present their findings. This hands-on, experiential approach helps student-teachers apply theoretical knowledge in real-world settings, encouraging them to construct their own understanding of child development.

One of the most prominent constructivist strategies used at Rahul College of Education is **Problem-Based Learning (PBL)**, where student-teachers are presented with complex, real-world problems that they must investigate and solve collaboratively. PBL challenges them to think critically, conduct research, and apply their knowledge to find solutions, rather than relying on memorization.In a course on educational policy, student-teachers might be tasked with developing a policy proposal for improving literacy rates in rural schools. They must research current educational practices, assess the needs of rural students, and propose innovative strategies to address the issue. Through this process, student-teachers construct their understanding of policy-making and gain valuable experience in problem-solving and critical thinking.

Constructivism also emphasizes the importance of **social interaction** in learning, aligning with **Vygotsky's Social Constructivism**, which suggests that learning is a collaborative process. At Rahul College of Education, group work, peer discussions, and collaborative projects are integral to the curriculum. Student-teachers learn by sharing ideas, challenging each other's thinking, and building on one another's insights. In a course on curriculum development, student-teachers work in groups to design a curriculum for a specific grade level and subject area. They must collaborate to identify learning objectives, select appropriate teaching methods, and create assessments. Through this collaborative process, they construct knowledge about curriculum design and gain insights into how collaborative learning can be applied in their future classrooms. **Inquiry-based learning** is another constructivist approach employed at Rahul College of Education. In this method, student-teachers are encouraged to ask questions, investigate topics, and seek out answers through exploration and research. Instead of being provided with direct answers, they engage in the learning process by exploring open-ended questions and discovering solutions on their own.In a course on environmental education, student-teachers might be asked to investigate the impact of climate change on local ecosystems. They conduct fieldwork, collect data, and analyze their findings to draw conclusions about the environmental issues at hand. This inquiry-based approach not only helps them construct knowledge about environmental science but also encourages them to think critically and become lifelong learners.

The faculty at Rahul College of Education are trained to use **constructivist teaching methods** that focus on guiding and facilitating learning rather than simply delivering content. Teachers act as facilitators who provide resources, pose questions, and support student-teachers in their learning journey. This student-centered approach empowers student-teachers to take ownership of their learning and develop the skills necessary to guide their future students in the same way.For instance, in a course on instructional strategies, faculty members might guide student- teachers through a project where they design and implement a lesson plan using constructivist methods. Instead of lecturing on the topic, faculty members provide resources, encourage experimentation, and offer feedback as student-teachers work through the process of creating their lessons. This approach mirrors how constructivist teaching methods will be applied in real classrooms, preparing student-teachers to foster active learning environments.

Constructivism in Practice

Micro-teaching is a key component of teacher education at Rahul College of Education, where student- teachers practice delivering lessons in a controlled environment before teaching in real classrooms. In the context of constructivism, student-teachers are encouraged to design micro- teaching sessions that promote active learning, inquiry, and collaboration among their peers. For example, a student-teacher might design a lesson on fractions for elementary students using manipulatives (physical objects) to help students construct an understanding of mathematical concepts. Instead of directly explaining how fractions work, the student-teacher might guide students through activities where they use manipulatives to explore the concept of fractions, encouraging them to make their own connections and discoveries.

In courses focused on lesson planning and instructional design, student-teachers at Rahul College of Education are tasked with developing constructivist lesson plans that emphasize active learning, inquiry, and real-world application. These lesson plans are designed to encourage students to engage with content in meaningful ways and construct their understanding through exploration and reflection. For instance, a student-teacher might develop a science lesson where middle school students conduct experiments to explore the properties of different materials. Instead of being told the results in advance, the students are encouraged to make predictions, test their hypotheses, and reflect on their findings, constructing their understanding of scientific principles through hands-on experience.

Reflection is a crucial element of constructivist learning at Rahul College of Education. Student-teachers are encouraged to engage in **reflective practice** by keeping journals where they document their learning experiences, challenges, and insights. Through reflective journaling, student-teachers are able to think critically about their own learning processes, identify areas for growth, and deepen their understanding of the material. For example, after completing a collaborative project, student-teachers might reflect on how their group dynamics influenced the learning process, what they learned from their peers, and how they can apply these insights in their future teaching. This reflective practice helps student-teachers internalize their learning and become more self-aware and adaptable educators. The constructivist approach at Rahul College of Education offers a progressive and student-centered learning environment that empowers future educators to thrive in their professional roles. Let's delve into the specific benefits that this approach brings to student-teachers

Constructivist learning emphasizes active engagement with the material, where student- teachers are not just passive receivers of information but are involved in the process of constructing their own understanding. At Rahul College of Education, student-teachers are encouraged to explore educational theories and practices through hands-on activities, discussions, and practical application in real-world contexts. This active involvement allows them to build deeper and more meaningful connections with the content. For example, rather than simply memorizing pedagogical theories, student-teachers are given opportunities to apply these theories through teaching simulations, classroom observations, and projects that mirror actual classroom dynamics. As a result, they gain a more profound understanding of how educational principles work in practice, which leads to a more effective teaching practice.

Constructivist learning at Rahul College of Education nurtures critical thinking skills by encouraging student-teachers to question existing assumptions, engage with diverse perspectives, and think creatively about problem-solving in education. In this approach, student-teachers are often presented with complex, open-ended questions or classroom challenges that do not have one right answer. By exploring multiple solutions, discussing with peers, and evaluating the strengths and weaknesses of various approaches, student-teachers develop the ability to think critically about educational issues. This skill is particularly valuable in teaching, where educators need to assess classroom situations, adapt to unexpected challenges, and make informed decisions that benefit their students. The constructivist approach helps student- teachers become reflective practitioners who can analyze their own teaching methods and continuously seek improvement.

Group work, peer discussions, and collaborative projects are central components of the constructivist approach at Rahul College of Education. These activities mirror the collaborative nature of teaching, where educators often work with colleagues, parents, and students to foster a productive learning environment. By engaging in collaborative learning experiences, student- teachers at Rahul College of Education develop strong communication and teamwork skills, which are essential for effective teaching. For instance, through group projects and peer-led discussions, student-teachers learn how to share ideas, listen to others' perspectives, and work together to solve common educational challenges. This collaboration also prepares them to create inclusive classrooms, where diverse opinions are respected, and students learn from one another.

One of the significant advantages of constructivist learning is that it encourages adaptability— a critical skill for future teachers. Education is an ever-evolving field, and student-teachersneed to be prepared to adjust their teaching strategies to meet the needs of diverse learners, changing curricula, and technological advancements. At Rahul College of Education, student-teachers engage in scenarios that require them to be flexible and responsive, such as adapting lesson plans based on classroom dynamics or utilizing new educational technologies. Constructivist learning fosters this adaptability by giving student-teachers the tools to experiment with different teaching approaches, reflect on their effectiveness, and refine their methods accordingly. By being adaptable, they are better equipped to create dynamic, student-centered learning environments in their future classrooms, where they can meet the individual needs of all students.

A core tenet of constructivism is the belief in the importance of continuous learning and self- improvement. At Rahul College of Education, student-teachers are encouraged to adopt a mindset of lifelong learning by engaging in reflective practices, inquiry-based learning, and professional development. Through reflection, student-teachers think critically about their teaching experiences, identify areas for growth, and set goals for their continued professional development. Inquiry-based learning allows them to explore new teaching methods, educational trends, and classroom innovations that can enhance their practice. This commitment to lifelong learning not only benefits the student-teachers during their time at Rahul College of Education but also ensures that they continue to evolve as educators throughout their careers. By instilling a passion for ongoing learning, the constructivist approach at Rahul College of Education helps student-teachers remain current, informed, and innovative in their teaching.

Conclusion: At Rahul College of Education, constructivism is not just a theoretical concept—it is a lived experience that shapes the way student-teachers learn and grow as future educators. By embracing constructivist principles such as active learning, collaboration, inquiry, and reflection, the college provides student-teachers with the tools they need to foster meaningful learning experiences in their own classrooms. Constructivism at Rahul College of Education empowers student-teachers to become thoughtful, reflective, and innovative educators who are equipped to meet the diverse needs of their future students.

References

- Fosnot, C.T., & Perry, R.S. (1996). "Constructivism: A Psychological Theory of Learning." In C.T. Fosnot (Ed.), *Constructivism: Theory, Perspectives, and Practice.* Teachers College Press.
- Piaget, J. (1950). *The Psychology of Intelligence.* Routledge.
- Vygotsky, L.S. (1978). *Mind in Society: The Development of Higher Psychological Processes.* Harvard University Press.

VI

Experiential Learning: Bridging Theory and Practice for Future Educators

"Experience is the teacher of all things."— *Julius Caesar*

Experiential learning is an educational approach that emphasizes learning through experience, reflection, and application. It focuses on the idea that knowledge is best gained when learners engage actively with real-world challenges and reflect on their experiences to derive meaning. At **Rahul College of Education**, experiential learning is a core component of teacher preparation, helping student-teachers bridge the gap between theoretical knowledge and practical application. By providing opportunities for hands-on learning, field experiences, and reflective practices, the college ensures that student-teachers are equipped with the skills and understanding necessary to become effective educators.

David Kolb's theory of **experiential learning** emphasizes learning through experience and is a foundational model for understanding how people learn in a hands-on, reflective, and iterative process. Kolb's four-stage cycle helps learners engage deeply with their learning experiences, connect them to theory, and apply them in new contexts.This model has four stages

Concrete Experience is the starting point of Kolb's experiential learning cycle. In this stage, learners engage in a direct experience, either in real life or through a simulation, where they actively participate in an event or activity. This experience could involve something as hands-on as conducting a science experiment, role-playing a classroom scenario, teaching a lesson, or participating in a field trip. The key to this stage is active involvement—learners are immersed in the moment and are fully experiencing the event. For example, in a teacher education program, student-teachers might visit a classroom to observe a lesson, or they might be tasked with delivering a mini-lesson themselves. This hands-on experience forms the foundation for the rest of the learning process, as it provides the raw material from which insights will be drawn.

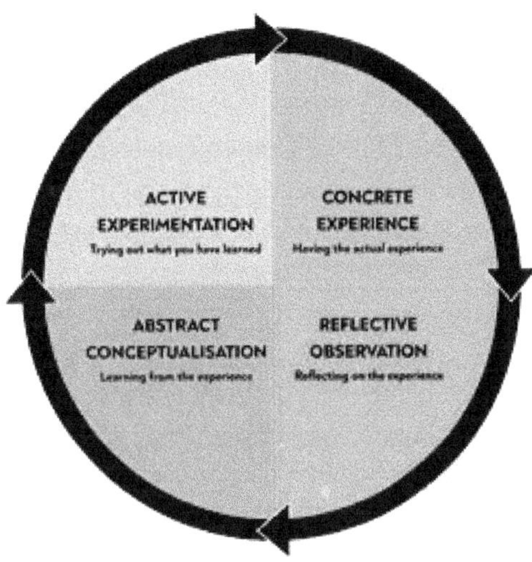

David Kolb's Theory ofExperiential Learning

After the experience, learners move to the **Reflective Observation** stage, where they think critically about what happened during the concrete experience. This is a time for introspection, where the learner takes a step back to observe and analyze the events. The focus is on observing

the results of the experience, considering the challenges, successes, and feelings encountered. Reflection can be done individually or through group discussion, and it is essential for learners to be honest and thoughtful during this process. For instance, a student-teacher who taught a lesson might reflect on how well they engaged the students, how they managed the classroom, or what could have been done differently. Through reflective observation, learners begin to make sense of their experience by identifying patterns, outcomes, and lessons learned, which forms the basis for deeper understanding.

In the **Abstract Conceptualization** stage, learners take the insights gained from reflection and begin to form broader concepts, theories, or principles. This is the stage where learners move beyond their immediate experience and use it to generate ideas that can be applied to future situations. In other words, they take what they've learned from their reflection and translate it into more generalizable knowledge or rules. This might involve connecting the experience to existing theories or developing new frameworks to understand similar experiences. For example, after reflecting on their teaching experience, a student-teacher might conclude that students learn best when they are actively engaged and may formulate a strategy to increase student participation in future lessons. In this stage, learners are synthesizing their concrete experience and reflection into abstract ideas that can guide future actions.

The final stage, **Active Experimentation**, involves applying the new knowledge or concepts to future situations. In this stage, learners test out the theories and strategies they developed during the Abstract Conceptualization phase. This might involve trying a new teaching method in the classroom, adjusting their communication style, or modifying a lesson plan based on their earlier reflections and ideas. Active experimentation completes the learning cycle, as the new experiences generated here can lead to further reflection and refinement, thus starting the cycle again. For example, a student-teacher might implement a new group activity strategy to see if it improves student engagement based on their previous experiences and reflections. This iterative process of applying, reflecting, conceptualizing, and experimenting fosters continuous growth and development.

The Cycle of Experiential Learning

The beauty of Kolb's model lies in its cyclical nature. Learning is not a one-time event but a continuous process where new experiences lead to new reflections, ideas, and actions. As learners continue to move through the cycle, they refine their understanding, gain deeper insights, and enhance their ability to apply what they have learned in a variety of contexts. For student-teachers, this ongoing process allows them to become more adaptive, reflective, and effective in their teaching practice.

Application in Education

In the context of teacher education, experiential learning can be especially valuable. By following Kolb's cycle, student-teachers can engage in real classroom experiences, reflect on their teaching, and then develop new strategies to apply in their future practice. This process helps them become more self-aware, confident, and capable educators. Additionally, experiential learning encourages lifelong learning, as teachers continue to learn and grow through their experiences in the classroom throughout their careers.In summary, Kolb's theory of experiential learning highlights the importance of experience, reflection, conceptualization, and experimentation in the learning process. This cycle empowers learners to derive meaning from their experiences, apply new insights to future challenges, and continually develop their skills and understanding.This process emphasizes the importance of reflection and active involvement, as learners develop insights from their experiences and use these insights to guide future actions. Experiential learning is learner-centered and encourages student-teachers to take an active role in constructing their own knowledge.

Experiential Learning in Practice

At Rahul College of Education, experiential learning is deeply integrated into the curriculum. Student-teachers are provided with numerous opportunities to engage in real-world teaching scenarios, interact with diverse learning environments, and reflect on their practices. The experiential learning process at Rahul College of Education not only focuses on practical skill development but also emphasizes self-awareness, adaptability, and continuous professional growth.

1. Teaching Practicum: Real-World Classroom Experience: The **teaching practicum** is one of the most important experiential learning components atRahul College of Education.

TIE AND DYE ACTIVITY- HANDS ON EXPERIENCE

During the practicum, student-teachers spend time working in real classrooms, applying the knowledge and skills they have gained in their coursework to actual teaching situations. This hands-on experience allows student-teachers to immerse themselves in the role of an educator and confront the challenges and rewards of teaching in a real-world context.A student-teacher might be placed in a school to teach a series of lessons in their subject area. They are responsible for planning lessons, managing the classroom, assessing student performance, and reflecting on their effectiveness as teachers. Throughout the practicum, faculty mentors from Rahul College of Education provide feedback and guidance, helping student-teachers refine their teaching strategies and address areas for improvement. By engaging in this immersive experience, student-teachers develop practical skills such as lesson planning, classroom management, differentiated instruction, and assessment techniques. Additionally, they gain a deeper understanding of how theoretical concepts from their coursework, such as learning theories and pedagogical approaches, apply in the classroom setting.

Microteaching is another important experiential learning strategy employed at Rahul College of Education. It provides student-teachers with the opportunity to practice teaching skills in a controlled and supportive environment before entering a full classroom. In microteaching sessions, student-teachers deliver short, focused lessons to their peers, who act as students. These sessions are often video-recorded, allowing for detailed feedback and self-reflection. For example, a student-teacher gets to conduct a 5-minute lesson on a specific topic, such as teaching a grammar rule in English. After delivering the lesson, the student-teacher receives feedback from their peers and faculty, who assess the effectiveness of their teaching strategies, use of teaching aids, communication skills, and classroom management techniques. The feedback allows the student-teacher to identify strengths and areas for improvement.

Microteaching offers a low-risk environment where student-teachers can experiment with different teaching methods, practice delivering content, and refine their instructional skills. It also fosters confidence and prepares student-teachers for the challenges of leading a full classroom.At Rahul College of Education, student-teachers are encouraged to conduct **action research projects** as part of their experiential learning journey. Action research involves identifying a problem or area for improvement in a classroom or school setting, implementing strategies to address the issue, and reflecting on the outcomes.

A student-teacher might conduct action research on improving student engagement in a science class. They might introduce new interactive teaching strategies, such as group projects or hands-on experiments, and then collect data on student participation and learning outcomes. After analyzing the data, the student-teacher reflects on the effectiveness of the strategies and makes adjustments for future lessons.This process allows student-teachers to engage in inquiry-based learning, develop problem- solving skills, and contribute to the improvement of teaching practices. It also fosters a mindset of continuous reflection and professional growth, as student-teachers learn to critically evaluate their own teaching methods.

Field trips and **educational visits** are also integral to the experiential learning approach at Rahul College of Education. These outings provide student-teachers with opportunities to observe different educational settings, explore new teaching environments, and gain insights into how education is delivered in various contexts.Student-teachers might visit a special education school to observe how teachers support students with diverse learning needs. During the visit, they interact with teachers, students, and administrators to learn about inclusive education practices and the challenges of working with students with disabilities. Such visits broaden student-teachers' understanding of the diverse learning environments they may encounter in their careers.

FIELD VISIT- FIRST HAND EXPERIENCE

Field trips are often followed by reflective discussions and assignments, where student-teachers analyze their experiences and consider how they can apply what they have learned to their own teaching practices. In today's digital age, **experiential learning** also extends to the use of technology. At Rahul College of Education, student-teachers engage with various digital tools and platforms to enhance their teaching and learning experiences. This includes designing and implementing lessons using interactive whiteboards, creating online learning environments, and utilizing educational apps to foster student engagement.Student-teachers may use simulation software to create virtual classroom scenarios where they can practice classroom management strategies or assess student learning. These digital tools provide an experiential learning platform that allows student-teachers to experiment with innovative teaching techniques in a simulated environment.

Service-learning is a key element of experiential learning at Rahul College of Education. Through **service-learning projects**, student-teachers work in partnership with local communities to address educational and social needs. These projects combine hands- on community service with reflective learning, helpingstudent-teachers apply their knowledge in real-world contexts while making a positive impact on the community.

OUTREACH ACTIVITY

Student-teachers organize a literacy campaign in a rural area, working with local schools and community organizations to develop reading programs for children.Throughout the project, they reflect on their experiences, assess the effectiveness of their strategies, and explore how education can be used as a tool for social change.Service-learning helps student-teachers develop a sense of social responsibility, cultural awareness, and empathy. It also reinforces the idea that education extends beyond the classroom and plays a vital role in community development and empowerment.

Reflection: A Crucial Component of Experiential Learning

Reflection is an essential part of experiential learning at Rahul College of Education. After each experience, whether it is a teaching practicum, microteaching session, or action research project, student-teachers are encouraged to reflect on their experiences through journals, discussions, and written reports. Reflection helps student-teachers make sense of their experiences, identify lessons learned, and consider how they can improve their teaching practices. By engaging in reflective practice, student-teachers develop a deeper understanding of their own learning processes and the impact of their teaching on student outcomes.For example, after completing a practicum, a student-teacher might write a reflective journal entry about how they handled a challenging classroom situation, such as managing disruptive behavior. Through reflection, they can evaluate what worked, what didn't, and how they might approach similar situations differently in the future.

Benefits of Experiential Learning

At Rahul College of Education, experiential learning provides student-teachers with opportunities to engage in practical, hands-on experiences that enhance their overall development as future educators. This approach allows them to gain real-world insights and build the essential skills they need to be effective teachers.

One of the most immediate and impactful benefits of experiential learning at Rahul College of Education is the development of practical teaching skills. By participating in teaching practicum, student- teachers have the chance to plan and deliver lessons, manage classrooms, and assess student learning in real-time. These experiences go beyond theoretical knowledge and allow student- teachers to face the actual challenges of a classroom environment. For example, through simulated lesson sessions, they can practice and refine skills such as engaging students, using technology in lessons, differentiating instruction for diverse learners, and addressing behavioral issues. This hands-on approach ensures that they are not just learning about these skills in theory but are applying them, getting feedback, and improving their techniques in a real-world setting. This experiential learning framework helps student-teachers transition smoothly from being learners to becoming competent educators.

Experiential learning bridges the gap between theory and practice, providing student-teachers with a deeper and more applied understanding of educational concepts. While classroom learning and reading about pedagogy offer foundational knowledge, applying that knowledge in real or simulated environments enables student-teachers to see how these theories work in practice. For instance, concepts such as constructivist teaching, differentiated instruction, and student-centered learning take on new meaning when student-teachers use them to design lessons or respond to students' needs in the classroom. When they see the impact of their strategies on student engagement and learning outcomes, theoretical concepts become more concrete, relevant, and meaningful. This practical application fosters critical thinking, as student-teachers must adapt educational theories to different contexts, varying student needs, and classroom realities. Experiential learning significantly boosts student-teachers' confidence and competence in their teaching abilities. Practical experiences, such as teaching practicums and microteaching, allow them to practice and refine their skills in a supportive environment. As they gain more experience in leading a classroom, handling diverse student behaviors, and experimenting with various teaching methods,they naturally become more confident in their capabilities. This confidence is crucial when transitioning to full-time teaching roles, as student-teachers will feel more prepared to face challenges and take charge of a classroom. Additionally, through feedback from mentors and peers, they can identify areas of improvement and celebrate their successes, reinforcing a sense of competence. This continuous process of trying, reflecting, and improving builds the resilience and self-assurance needed to excel as educators.

Reflection is a cornerstone of experiential learning at Rahul College of Education, encouraging student- teachers to engage in reflective practice to continuously improve their teaching. After each teaching experience—whether it's a lesson they taught, a classroom they observed, or a service- learning project they participated in—student-teachers are encouraged to reflect on their performance. This reflection might involve considering questions such as: What went well? What challenges did I face? How did students respond? What could I do differently next time? This reflective practice helps student-teachers develop self-awareness and critical thinking skills as they analyze their strengths and areas for growth. It also fosters a habit of continuous professional development, as teachers who reflect on their practice are more likely to seek out new strategies, resources, and ideas for improving their teaching. By developing this reflective mindset early in their careers, student-teachers at Rahul College of Education are better equipped to grow and evolve as educators over time.

Through experiential learning projects, particularly those that involve service-learning and community engagement, student-teachers at Rahul College of Education are exposed to the social and cultural dynamics of education. These projects often involve working with diverse communities, understanding the needs of underprivileged students, and contributing to socially responsible causes. By participating in these activities, student-teachers develop a deeper sense of empathy and social awareness. They come to understand the role that teachers play not just in the classroom, but in shaping society as a whole. For example, a service-learning project might involve teaching literacy to children from disadvantaged backgrounds or organizing community outreach programs in local schools. These experiences foster a sense of social responsibility, helping student-teachers recognize the impact of education on broader societal issues and preparing them to be educators who are not only focused on academic outcomes but also on the holistic well-being and development of their students.

In summary, the experiential learning approach at Rahul College of Education offers student- teachers a comprehensive and practical path to becoming skilled, reflective, and socially conscious educators. Through real-world teaching experiences, reflective practice, and service- learning, they develop essential skills, deepen their understanding of educational theory, build confidence, and become adaptive and empathetic educators. This approach ensures that student-teachers are not only prepared to succeed in their classrooms but also equipped to contribute meaningfully to their communities and the education profession.

Conclusion

At Rahul College of Education, experiential learning is a fundamental approach that empowers student-teachers to become reflective, skilled, and socially responsible educators. Through hands-on experiences, fieldwork, reflective practice, and community engagement, student- teachers develop the practical skills and theoretical understanding necessary to excel in their teaching careers. By integrating experiential learning into its curriculum, Rahul College of Education prepares future educators to navigate the complexities of the classroom and contribute meaningfully to the field of education.

References:

- Kolb, D.A. (1984). *Experiential Learning: Experience as the Source of Learning and Development.* Prentice-Hall.
- Dewey, J. (1938). *Experience and Education.* Kappa Delta Pi.
- Beard, C., & Wilson, J.P. (2013). *Experiential Learning: A Handbook for Education, Training, and Coaching.* Kogan Page Publishers.

VII

Cooperative Learning: Fostering Collaboration, Communication, Critical Thinking

"Coming together is a beginning, staying together is progress, and working together is success."— *Henry Ford*

Cooperative learning is an instructional strategy that emphasizes collaboration among students to achieve common learning goals. At **Rahul College of Education**, cooperative learning is a key pedagogical approach used to prepare student-teachers for the dynamic and interactive nature of the teaching profession. It encourages teamwork, enhances communication skills, and promotes critical thinking, all of which are essential qualities for future educators. Cooperative learning not only fosters a sense of community within the classroom but also mirrors real-world teaching environments, where collaboration among educators, students, and communities is crucial.

Cooperative learning is based on the principle that students learn best when they work together, share ideas, and support each other's learning. In cooperative learning, small groups of students work towards a common academic goal, with each member contributing to the group's success. This approach shifts the focus from individual competition to collective achievement, encouraging students to rely on each other's strengths and to support one another's learning. Cooperative learning is an instructional strategy that involves students working together in small groups to achieve a common goal, fostering both academic and social development. Let's explore the key elements of cooperative learning in more detail:

This element refers to the idea that group members are linked together in such a way that one cannot succeed unless all group members succeed. This creates a sense of mutual support and encourages collaboration rather than competition. In positive interdependence, students recognize that their success depends on the collective effort of the group, which promotes cooperation and shared responsibility. For example, in a project-based task, each member might be assigned a specific role or task, but the final outcome relies on everyone completing their part. This can be achieved through shared goals, resources, or rewards, ensuring that all members contribute to the group's success.Even though students work in groups, each member is accountable for their own learning and contribution. This ensures that no one "coasts" on the work of others. Teachers often assess both individual and group performance to maintain individual accountability. Techniques such as quizzes, peer evaluations, or requiring students to present their part of a project can help ensure that everyone is doing their fair share. This prevents "free riding," where one or two members do all the work while others benefit without contributing. Individual accountability also motivates students to engage fully, knowing their effort is vital to both their own and the group's success.

Cooperative learning emphasizes direct interaction among group members. This interaction allows students to exchange ideas, provide feedback, and offer support to one another. Face- to-face interaction is important because it fosters communication and allows for the development of interpersonal skills. During this interaction, students explain their reasoning, listen to their peers, ask questions, and clarify understanding, leading to deeper learning.

Group discussions, brainstorming sessions, and problem-solving activities are examples where students benefit from interacting directly with one another.

For cooperative learning to be successful, students must develop and use a range of social and teamwork skills. These collaborative skills include communication, leadership, conflict resolution, active listening, negotiation, and decision-making. Students must learn how to share ideas, give and receive feedback constructively, and manage differences of opinion. Teachers often need to explicitly teach these skills, as they are not always inherent. Activities that encourage teamwork, such as role-playing conflict resolution scenarios or structuring group decision-making processes, help students enhance these skills. Developing collaborative skills not only benefits students academically but also prepares them for real-world situations where teamwork is essential.

Group processing involves reflecting on group performance to improve future collaboration. It allows groups to evaluate how effectively they worked together, what went well, and what could be improved. This self-assessment is crucial for improving the group dynamic and ensuring that members are learning from their experiences. Group processing can be facilitated through discussions, where members talk about their individual and collective efforts, or through structured tools like group reflection forms. During this process, students can also address any issues they encountered, such as unequal participation, and develop strategies to overcome them in the future. Group processing promotes continuous improvement and helps students become more effective collaborators over time. Cooperative learning fosters an environment where students work together toward common goals, but success is contingent upon both group collaboration and individual contributions. Through positive interdependence, accountability, direct interaction, collaborative skill development, and group reflection, students not only learn academic content but also develop crucial social skills and a deeper understanding of working effectively in teams.

Cooperative Learning in Practice at Rahul College of Education

At Rahul College of Education, cooperative learning is integrated into various courses and activities, preparing student-teachers to use this approach in their future classrooms. By participating in cooperative learning activities, student-teachers not only gain content knowledge but also develop the skills necessary to foster collaboration and teamwork among their future students.

Cooperative Learning at Rahul College of Education

One of the most common ways cooperative learning is implemented at Rahul College of Education is through **group projects** and **collaborative lesson planning**. Student-teachers are assigned to small groups where they work together to create lesson plans, design instructional materials, or develop classroom management strategies. Each group member is responsible for contributing to the project, and the success of the group depends on the collective efforts of all participants. For example, in a course on instructional design, student-teachers might be assigned a project where they must create a unit plan for a specific subject and grade level. Each member of the group is tasked with researching different aspects of the unit, such as learning objectives, instructional methods, and assessment strategies. Group members then bring their ideas together to create a cohesive, well-rounded unit plan that reflects the input and expertise of all members. This process not only encourages collaboration but also helps student-teachers learn how to divide responsibilities, communicate effectively, and integrate diverse perspectives into their teaching practices.

The **jigsaw method** is a cooperative learning strategy frequently used at Rahul College of Education. In this approach, each student-teacher is assigned a specific portion of a topic to research and become an "expert" on. After completing their individual research, student-teachers return to their groups to share their expertise, teaching their peers about their portion of the topic. In this way, each group member contributes a vital piece of knowledge to the collective understanding of the subject.

In Teaching and Learning course, the student-teachers use the jigsaw method to explore different learning theories, such as constructivism, behaviourism, and cognitivism. Each group member is responsible for researching one theory, and then they come together to teach their peers about the key concepts, applications, and classroom implications of each theory. This approach not only deepens individual understanding of the topic but also promotes active listening and mutual respect among peers. By using the jigsaw method, Rahul College of Education encourages positive interdependence, as each group member's contribution is essential for the success of the group. It also fosters a sense of responsibility, as student-teachers know that their peers are relying on them to provide accurate and relevant information.

At Rahul College of Education, **peer teaching** is an important cooperative learning strategy that allows student-teachers to collaborate on lesson delivery and engage in reflective discussions about teaching practices. In peer teaching activities, student-teachers take turns leading lessons or presenting content, while their peers provide feedback and suggestions for improvement. This approach not only promotes collaboration but also helps student-teachers practice their teaching skills in a supportive environment.In a course on classroom management, student-teachers might work in pairs to design and deliver a lesson on managing student behavior. After one student-teacher presents the lesson, their partner provides constructive feedback, offering insights into what worked well and what could be improved. This feedback is then discussed, allowing both participants to reflect on their teaching strategies and make adjustments for future lessons.

Peer teaching fosters a culture of collaboration and mutual support, where student-teachers learn from each other's strengths and offer guidance to improve overall teaching effectiveness.During their **teaching practicum**, student-teachers at Rahul College of Education often engage in cooperative learning by collaborating with mentor teachers, fellow student-teachers, and school staff. These collaborations help student-teachers apply cooperative learning principles in realclassroom settings, working together to plan lessons, manage classrooms, and assess student learning.For example, during a practicum placement in a primary school, a group of student-teachers might be assigned to co-teach a unit on environmental science. Working together, they divide the responsibilities for lesson planning, instructional delivery, and assessment. One student- teacher might lead an interactive activity on ecosystems, while another facilitates a group discussion on conservation practices. By sharing responsibilities and supporting one another, student-teachers experience the power of cooperative teaching and how it can benefit both educators and students.This real-world application of cooperative learning helps student-teachers develop teamwork skills, build professional relationships, and understand the value of collaboration in a school setting.

At Rahul College of Education, cooperative learning is also used to promote **problem-solving and critical thinking**. Student-teachers are frequently presented with complex, real-world educational problems that they must solve collaboratively. These problems often require student-teachers to think critically, consider multiple perspectives, and work together to develop innovative solutions.For example, in a course on inclusive education, student-teachers might be asked to work in groups to develop strategies for supporting students with diverse learning needs in a mainstream classroom. Each group must consider factors such as differentiated instruction, classroom accommodations, and communication with parents. Through group discussions and collaborative brainstorming, student-teachers develop a range of solutions that they present to the class.This approach not only encourages deep thinking and creativity but also reinforces the importance of collaboration in addressing the challenges of teaching in diverse and inclusive classrooms.

Examples of Cooperative Learning at Rahul College of Education

In a course on educational research, student-teachers participate in **group-based inquiry projects** where they work together to design, conduct, and present research on an educational topic. For example, a group might investigate the impact of technology on student engagement in the classroom. Each group member is responsible for gathering data, analyzing results, and contributing to the final research report. This cooperative learning experience not only helps student-teachers develop research skills but also fosters teamwork and collective problem- solving. As part of their teacher training, student-teachers at Rahul College of Education work in teams to create **collaborative curriculum units** for various subjects. These projects require student-teachers to pool their knowledge and expertise to design comprehensive units that include lesson plans, assessments, and instructional materials. For example, a team might create a curriculum unit on global citizenship that incorporates social studies, language arts, and project-based learning. Through this collaborative process, student-teachers learn how to integrate different subjects and teaching methods while working together to achieve a common goal.

Rahul College of Education also integrates **service-learning projects** into its cooperative learning framework. Student-teachers work in teams to organize community-based service projects, such as running after-school tutoring programs or organizing literacy workshops for underserved populations. These cooperative projects help student-teachers develop leadership and teamwork skills while contributing to the community.

Benefits of Cooperative Learning

Cooperative learning offers a powerful and transformative learning experience for student- teachers at institutions like Rahul College of Education. By working in groups, student-teachers not only master subject matter but also develop essential skills for their future roles as educators. Effective communication is a cornerstone of teaching, and cooperative learning provides student-teachers with ample opportunities to improve this skill. In group settings, student- teachers must articulate their ideas, listen to others, and engage in discussions to reach common goals.

This interaction helps them refine their ability to express complex concepts clearly, respond to questions, and present their viewpoints in an organized manner. Regular participation in group discussions also boosts their confidence in public speaking, an essential aspect of teaching. For instance, when student-teachers explain a concept to their peers, they practice simplifying content and ensuring clarity, which directly translates to classroom communication skills.

Cooperative learning fosters a strong sense of collaboration and teamwork, skills that are indispensable in the field of education. Student-teachers learn to work with diverse individuals, accommodating different perspectives, learning styles, and ideas. This diversity prepares them to collaborate with colleagues, parents, and administrators in their future teaching careers. By sharing responsibilities in a group setting, they also learn to divide tasks based on strengths, manage group dynamics, and achieve common goals. These experiences mirror the collaborative nature of teaching, where educators must work together to design curricula, solve classroom issues, and support student learning.

Group work encourages student-teachers to engage in higher-order thinking. When faced with complex problems, they are challenged to think critically, analyze different perspectives, and synthesize information to come up with solutions. Collaborative discussions push them to evaluate the validity of their ideas, consider alternative viewpoints, and refine their problem-solving strategies. This process of collective brainstorming and critical analysis helps them develop innovative and well-rounded solutions. In a real-world classroom, this translates to the ability to tackle educational challenges—such as differentiating instruction for diverse learners or finding new approaches to engage students—using a critical and solution-oriented mindset.

Cooperative learning also promotes positive social interactions, which are crucial for building a supportive and inclusive educational environment. As student-teachers work together, they learn to resolve conflicts, negotiate differences, and build strong working relationships. This experience of navigating social dynamics prepares them to manage classroom interactions with students and collaborate effectively with colleagues. Moreover, by supporting each other's learning, student-teachers foster a sense of camaraderie and mutual respect. These interactions help them develop empathy, patience, and understanding—qualities that are essential for building positive teacher-student relationships in their future classrooms.

In cooperative learning, each student-teacher is accountable for their own contributions to the group's success. This sense of individual responsibility helps them understand the importance of being reliable and proactive. By taking ownership of their tasks, they develop a strong work ethic and learn the value of contributing meaningfully to the group. At the same time, cooperative learning reinforces the idea of mutual support. Student-teachers must not only complete their own tasks but also ensure that their peers are equally supported and successful. This fosters a sense of shared responsibility, where success is measured by the group's collective achievement rather than individual accomplishments. In their future teaching careers, this prepares them for the collaborative nature of working in educational teams and school communities.

Real-World Application

Perhaps one of the most significant benefits of cooperative learning for student-teachers is its direct application to the real world. In classrooms, educators often work collaboratively with other teachers, administrators, parents, and support staff to create a positive learning environment for students. Through cooperative learning experiences, student-teachers get a practical understanding of how to work in teams, co-plan lessons, and share responsibilities in an educational setting. This experience also reinforces the importance of peer learning and collaboration in the classroom—concepts they can apply when designing group activities for their future students. As student-teachers experience firsthand the benefits of collaborative learning, they are more likely to implement similar strategies in their classrooms, promoting a cooperative and inclusive learning environment for their students.

In summary, cooperative learning equips student-teachers at Rahul College of Education with a range of skills that are critical for both their personal and professional development. By enhancing communication, collaboration, critical thinking, and social interaction, while also fostering accountability and preparing them for the realities of teamwork in education, cooperative learning ensures that student-teachers are well-prepared to succeed in the collaborative and dynamic environment of modern education.

Conclusion

Cooperative learning is a vital component of teacher education at Rahul College of Education, preparing student-teachers to become collaborative, communicative, and reflective educators.Through group projects, peer teaching, collaborative problem-solving, and real-world field experiences, student-teachers develop the skills and mindset necessary to foster cooperation and teamwork in their future classrooms. Cooperative learning not only enhances academic achievement but also builds a sense of community and mutual respect among future educators, setting the stage for successful and fulfilling teaching careers.

References

- Johnson, D.W., & Johnson, R.T. (1999). *Learning Together and Alone: Cooperative, Competitive, and Individualistic Learning.* Allyn and Bacon.
- Gillies, R.M. (2007). *Cooperative Learning: Integrating Theory and Practice.* SAGE Publications.
- Kagan, S. (1994). *Cooperative Learning.* Kagan Publishing

VIII

Technology-Enhanced Learning: A 21st Century Approach to Teacher Education

The real problem is not whether machines think but whether men do."— *B.F. Skinner*

In the rapidly evolving educational landscape of the 21st century, technology plays a crucial role in enhancing teaching and learning processes. At **Rahul College of Education**, technology-enhanced learning (TEL) is embraced as an essential component of teacher preparation, ensuring that student-teachers are equipped with the skills and knowledge necessary to integrate technology into their future classrooms. Through various digital tools, online resources, and innovative learning platforms, the college empowers student-teachers to become proficient in using technology to improve educational outcomes and foster an engaging, interactive learning environment.

TECHNOLOGY ENHANCED LEARNING

Technology-enhanced learning refers to the use of technology to support, supplement, or transform the learning process. TEL includes a wide range of digital tools and strategies that facilitate teaching and learning, from basic applications such as interactive whiteboards and presentation software to advanced innovations like virtual simulations, online collaboration platforms, and artificial intelligence (AI)-driven learning systems.The integration of technology in education brings a host of benefits that are transforming the learning experience for student-teachers, particularly at institutions like Rahul College of Education. By leveraging digital tools and platforms, student-teachers are not only enhancing their learning but also developing skills that will be essential in the modern classroom. Let's elaborate on each of the points:

One of the most significant advantages of using digital tools in education is their ability to enhance student engagement. Interactive tools like digital whiteboards, educational apps, and multimedia resources such as videos, simulations, and gamified learning experiences make learning more dynamic and immersive. These resources help bring abstract concepts to life, making lessons more relatable and accessible. For instance, in a lesson on biology, student- teachers could use a virtual lab to explore cellular processes, which provides a far more engaging experience than merely reading about it in a textbook. The visual and interactive elements grab students' attention, keep them actively involved, and cater to different learning styles, which can significantly improve retention and understanding.

Technology facilitates collaboration by enabling student-teachers to connect with peers, mentors, and experts beyond the traditional classroom walls. Online platforms, such as learning management systems (LMS), discussion forums, and collaborative tools like Google Docs, allow student-teachers to work together on group projects, share ideas, and engage in discussions, even when they are not physically together. This fosters a collaborative learning environment where ideas can be exchanged freely, and feedback can be provided in real-time. Collaboration tools encourage teamwork, peer learning, and the development of communication skills, which are critical for future educators. In teacher education programs, for example, student-teachers might collaborate on lesson planning or problem-solving exercises through online platforms, simulating the type of collaborative work they will need to do with colleagues in their future schools.

Adaptive learning technologies enable a more personalized learning experience by providing student-teachers with tailored feedback and support based on their individual progress and needs. These technologies use data analytics and artificial intelligence to monitor a student's learning patterns, identify strengths and areas for improvement, and adjust the content or pace accordingly. For example, in a teacher education program, an adaptive learning platform might identify that a student-teacher struggles with classroom management strategies and then offer targeted resources, quizzes, or simulations to address this gap. Personalization helps ensure that each learner receives the specific guidance and resources they need to succeed, making the learning experience more efficient and effective. It also allows student-teachers to progress at their own pace, ensuring they fully understand the material before moving on to more advanced concepts.

Digital platforms dramatically expand access to educational resources, making it easier for student-teachers to explore a wealth of content that would otherwise be difficult to obtain. Through these platforms, student-teachers can access academic journals, e-books, online courses, videos, and various multimedia materials. For instance, through platforms like Google Scholar or institutional access to databases like JSTOR, student-teachers can stay updated with the latest research in education. Additionally, open educational resources (OER) provide free access to high-quality teaching materials that student-teachers can use to develop their own lessons. This increased access empowers student-teachers to broaden their learning, stay current on emerging trends, and deepen their understanding of key topics in education. It also fosters independent learning and research, encouraging student-teachers to become resourceful educators who can continue learning and evolving throughout their careers.

In the 21st-century classroom, digital literacy is a crucial skill for both teachers and students. By incorporating technology into their own learning, student-teachers at institutions like Rahul College of Education are trained to use digital tools effectively and responsibly. This includes understanding how to integrate technology into lesson plans, use digital platforms for assessment and feedback, and engage students with various digital resources. Importantly, digital literacy also involves understanding the ethical use of technology, including issues related to data privacy, copyright, and cyber safety. By developing these skills, student-teachers are prepared to meet the demands of the digital age of education, where technology is increasingly becoming an integral part of teaching and learning. Furthermore, by becoming proficient in digital literacy themselves, student-teachers will be better equipped to teach these skills to their future students, ensuring that they are also prepared to thrive in a digitally connected world.

At Rahul College of Education, TEL is seamlessly integrated into both the curriculum and the overall learning environment. Student-teachers engage with various forms of technology to enhance their understanding of pedagogy, content delivery, and classroom management. TEL is not just about using technology for the sake of it, but about how technology can improve learning outcomes, foster deeper understanding, and prepare future educators to navigate the challenges of a digital classroom.

One of the foundational elements of TEL at Rahul College of Education is the use of a **Learning Management System (LMS)**, which serves as a central platform for managing course content, assignments, and communication between students and faculty. Through the LMS, student- teachers can access course materials, submit assignments, participate in discussions, and receive feedback from instructors. For example, student-teachers might be assigned to complete an online quiz on teaching methods, upload lesson plans for peer review, or participate in discussion forums where they analyze case studies on classroom management. The LMS not only streamlines these processes but also provides a digital space for student- teachers to engage in collaborative learning and reflective practice.

The LMS also supports **blended learning** by combining face-to-face instruction with online activities. For instance, student-teachers might attend a lecture on curriculum design and then complete an online module that includes multimedia resources, such as instructional videos or interactive diagrams, to reinforce key concepts.

At Rahul College of Education, **interactive whiteboards** are a standard feature in classrooms, allowing instructors and student-teachers to create dynamic, interactive lessons. These boards combine traditional teaching methods with digital tools, enabling instructors to display multimedia content, annotate materials, and engage students in real-time discussions. For example, during a lesson on educational psychology, the instructor might use an interactive whiteboard to display a video illustrating a learning theory. Student-teachers can then annotate the video with their observations, engage in a group discussion about the implications of the theory, and save the annotations for future reference. This interactive approach fosters a deeper understanding of the subject matter and encourages active participation.

Additionally, **digital classrooms** at Rahul College of Education are equipped with advanced technologies, such as projectors, smart devices, and high-speed internet, which provide student-teachers with access to a variety of online tools and resources. These classrooms simulate the digital learning environments that student-teachers are likely to encounter in modern schools, helping them become comfortable with using technology as part of their teaching practice. Incorporating **virtual simulations** and **augmented reality (AR)** into teacher training is another way Rahul College of Education enhances learning through technology. These tools provide student- teachers with immersive, interactive experiences that replicate real-world teaching scenarios, allowing them to practice their skills in a controlled environment.For example, student-teachers might participate in a virtual classroom simulation where they practice classroom management techniques, such as handling student misbehavior or facilitating group work. These simulations provide instant feedback, helping student-teachers refine their strategies and build confidence in their teaching abilities. Similarly, AR can be used to enhance subjects such as science education. Student-teachers might use AR apps to visualize complex concepts, such as the structure of the human body or the solar system, in a three-dimensional space. This not only makes learning more engaging but also helps student-teachers understand how to incorporate such technologies into their own teaching.

Rahul College of Education encourages the use of the **flipped classroom** model, where traditional lecture- based instruction is reversed. In this model, student-teachers are given access to instructional materials, such as videos, readings, or podcasts, before class. During in-class time, they engage in collaborative activities, discussions, and problem-solving tasks based on the material they studied independently.For example, before a lesson on inclusive education, student-teachers might be assigned a video on differentiated instruction. After watching the video at home, they come to class prepared to discuss the content and work on case studies where they apply the concepts to real classroom situations. This model fosters self-directed learning, critical thinking, and the ability to apply theoretical knowledge to practical challenges.By flipping the classroom, Rahul College of Education shifts the focus from passive learning to active engagement, where student-teachers take ownership of their learning process and work collaboratively to solve problems and develop teaching strategies.

To facilitate **collaborative learning** and communication, Rahul College of Education utilizes a range of online tools, such as **Google Classroom, Zoom, Microsoft Teams,** and **Slack**. These platforms enable student-teachers to work together on group projects, share resources, and communicate with instructors and peers in real-time, regardless of geographical location.For example, student-teachers working on a group assignment might use Google Docs to collaborate on a shared document, where each member contributes their part of the project. They can also use Zoom or Microsoft Teams to conduct virtual meetings, where they discuss their progress and divide responsibilities. This collaborative use of technology mirrors the digital collaboration tools that educators are increasingly using in schools, preparing student- teachers to work effectively in a tech-driven environment. Additionally, online discussion forums and messaging platforms allow student-teachers to engage in asynchronous discussions about course content. This enables deeper reflection, as student-teachers have time to think critically about their responses and engage in meaningful dialogue with their peers.

Technology at Rahul College of Education also enhances the **assessment and feedback** process. Digital tools allow for more efficient, timely, and personalized feedback, enabling student-teachers to track their progress and identify areas for improvement. Online quizzes, interactive assessments, and automated grading systems are frequently used to provide immediate feedback on student-teachers' performance. For example, after completing an online quiz on classroom management strategies, student- teachers receive instant feedback on their answers, along with explanations of the correct responses. This immediate feedback helps reinforce learning and allows student-teachers to reflect on their understanding of the material.

In addition, instructors at Rahul College of Education use digital platforms to provide detailed, personalized feedback on assignments. They can annotate student-teachers' work directly in the digital submission, highlighting areas of strength and suggesting improvements. This approach fosters a deeper connection between instructors and students, while also helping student-teachers improve their practice based on constructive feedback.Rahul College of Education encourages student-teachers to participate in **Massive Open Online Courses (MOOCs)** and use **Open Educational Resources (OERs)** to enhance their learning. MOOCs, offered by platforms such as Coursera, edX, and Future Learn, provide student-teachers with opportunities to explore topics beyond the college curriculum, such as emerging trends in education, new teaching methods, or subject-specific content.For example, a student-teacher interested in digital literacy might enrol in a MOOC on integrating technology into the classroom. By completing the course, they gain valuable insights and practical skills that they can apply to their future teaching practice.

Similarly, OERs, such as free textbooks, lesson plans, and multimedia resources, allow student- teachers to access high-quality educational materials without cost barriers. This democratization of knowledge supports continuous professional development and encourages student-teachers to stay informed about the latest advancements in education.One of the core goals of TEL at Rahul College of Education is to develop **digital literacy** among student-teachers. Digital literacy goes beyond knowing how to use technology; it involves understanding how to use technology ethically, critically, and creatively in educational settings.For example, student-teachers are trained to evaluate the credibility of online resources, design interactive digital content, and teach students about online safety and digital citizenship. These skills are essential for educators in the 21st century, as technology becomes increasingly integrated into all aspects of education.

Technology-Enhanced Learning (TEL) significantly transforms the educational experience for student-teachers at Rahul College of Education. By incorporating various digital tools and resources into their studies, student-teachers can enjoy numerous benefits that not only enhance their learning but also prepare them for their future careers in education. Interactive technologies play a crucial role in making learning more engaging for student-teachers. Digital tools such as simulations, educational games, and interactive multimedia presentations capture attention and stimulate interest, turning traditional lessons into dynamic learning experiences. When student-teachers actively participate in their learning—whether through interactive quizzes, gamified assignments, or virtual classrooms—they tend to retain information better and maintain higher motivation levels. This engagement is especially vital in teacher education, as it models the kind of active learning approaches that student-teachers will later use in their own classrooms. By experiencing engaging learning methods first hand, they are more likely to implement similar strategies with their future students.

Digital platforms significantly broaden the scope of resources available to student-teachers, allowing them to explore subjects in greater depth and breadth. Online libraries, academic databases, and educational websites provide access to a plethora of scholarly articles, e-books, research studies, and teaching materials. This wealth of resources empowers student-teachers to conduct thorough research, stay updated on educational trends, and develop a more comprehensive understanding of their subjects. For instance, they might access video lectures from leading educators, attend virtual workshops, or collaborate on research projects with peers from other institutions. This access not only enriches their learning experience but also helps them cultivate a habit of lifelong learning, which is essential in the constantly evolving field of education.One of the standout features of TEL is its ability to facilitate personalized learning experiences. Adaptive learning technologies tailor educational content and feedback to meet the specific needs of individual learners. For student-teachers, this means they can progress through material at their own pace, revisiting challenging concepts or advancing quickly through topics they grasp easily. Such personalized approaches ensure that each student-teacher receives the support they need to succeed. For example, if a student-teacher struggles with classroom management strategies, adaptive learning platforms can offer targeted exercises, resources, and assessments to help them improve. This individualized feedback fosters a more effective learning environment and ensures that student-teachers feel empowered in their educational journey.

TEL enhances collaboration among student-teachers through various online tools and platforms. Technologies such as discussion forums, group chats, and collaborative document editing allow student-teachers to work together seamlessly, regardless of physical location. This collaboration is essential in teacher education, as it helps student-teachers develop important teamwork and communication skills that are vital for their future roles as educators. For instance, they might collaborate on lesson planning, share insights on best practices, or engage in peer reviews of each other's teaching materials. Such collaborative experiences not only enrich their learning but also model the collaborative practices they will encounter in their professional lives.

Integrating technology into teacher education equips student-teachers with the skills and confidence to use digital tools effectively in their future classrooms. Familiarity with various educational technologies enables them to enhance their teaching methods, engage students more effectively, and facilitate interactive learning experiences. This preparation is crucial as classrooms increasingly incorporate technology into daily teaching practices. Student-teachers who are comfortable with technology will be better positioned to create dynamic, tech-infused learning environments that resonate with digital-native students. Furthermore, by experiencing how technology can enhance education, student-teachers are more likely to advocate for its effective use in their own future teaching contexts.

Technology-Enhanced Learning fosters the development of essential 21st-century skills that are crucial for success in the modern educational landscape. Through TEL, student-teachers hone skills such as digital literacy, which encompasses the ability to effectively navigate and evaluate information from various digital sources. Additionally, they develop critical thinking and problem-solving skills as they engage with complex educational challenges through simulations and online discussions. Creativity is also nurtured as student-teachers explore innovative ways to present information and engage learners using technology. These skills are not only vital for their success as teachers but also for preparing their students to thrive in an increasingly complex and digital world.

Conclusion

Technology-enhanced learning is a cornerstone of teacher education at Rahul College of Education, preparing student-teachers to navigate the digital age of education. By integrating digital tools, online platforms, and innovative teaching strategies into the curriculum, Rahul College of Education equips future educators with the skills and knowledge they need to create engaging, effective, and technologically enriched learning environments. Through TEL, student-teachers not only enhance their own learning but also gain the confidence and expertise to use technology to inspire and educate the next generation of learners.

References

- Selwyn, N. (2011). *Education and Technology: Key Issues and Debates.* Bloomsbury Publishing
- Bates, A.W. (2019). *Teaching in a Digital Age: Guidelines for Designing Teaching and Learning.* Tony Bates Associates.
- Mayer, R.E. (2001). *Multimedia Learning.* Cambridge University Press.

IX

Learning Through Indian Knowledge Systems: A Pathway to Holistic Teacher Development

"Education is not the filling of a pail, but the lighting of a fire."— *William Butler Yeats*

Indian Knowledge Systems (IKS), deeply rooted in the diverse cultural, philosophical, and scientific heritage of India, offer a unique and holistic approach to learning. At **Rahul College of Education**, learning through Indian Knowledge Systems is integrated into the teacher education curriculum to foster a connection with traditional wisdom while preparing future educators for the demands of modern education. This approach emphasizes the richness of India's intellectual traditions and their relevance to contemporary education, creating well- rounded educators who can draw upon both indigenous knowledge and modern pedagogical practices.

Indian Knowledge Systems encompass a wide array of disciplines, including philosophy, science, arts, architecture, medicine, education, and ethics, developed over centuries in India. These systems are based on a holistic worldview, emphasizing the interconnectedness of all life, the importance of ethics and values, and the pursuit of knowledge for personal growth, societal well-being, and environmental sustainability.

At Rahul College of Education, the integration of Indigenous Knowledge Systems (IKS) is not merely about preserving traditional knowledge; it is a transformative educational philosophy that emphasizes a holistic approach to teaching and learning. This approach nurtures various dimensions of student-teachers' growth and development.

The philosophy of IKS at Rahul College of Education prioritizes holistic development, recognizing that education extends beyond cognitive learning to encompass the mind, body, and spirit. This perspective acknowledges the interconnectedness of intellectual, emotional, physical, and spiritual growth. For student-teachers, this means engaging in a curriculum that fosters a well- rounded development. For instance, alongside academic learning, they may participate in physical activities like yoga, which promotes physical well-being and mindfulness. Similarly, spiritual development may be fostered through practices such as meditation, which encourages self-awareness and emotional regulation. By addressing these multiple dimensions, IKS prepares student-teachers to develop into compassionate and balanced educators who can support the diverse needs of their future students.

IKS emphasizes ethical and value-based learning by instilling core values such as respect, compassion, and responsibility. At Rahul College of Education, this means embedding these values into the curriculum and teaching practices. Student-teachers are encouraged to reflect on their own values and how these impact their role as educators. This can be done through discussions, case studies, and community engagement projects that challenge them to consider ethical dilemmas in education. By fostering an environment that prioritizes respect for diverse cultures and perspectives, student-teachers learn the importance of inclusivity and equity in their classrooms. Moreover, as they cultivate compassion and responsibility, they are better equipped to model these values for their students, ultimately creating a positive and nurturing classroom environment.

Rahul College of Education also promotes a sense of community and environmental responsibility. By understanding the interconnectedness of human beings and the natural world, student-teachers are encouraged to recognize their role within their communities and the larger ecosystem. This can involve participation in community service projects, where they engage with local populations, learn about community needs, and contribute to social well-being. Additionally, environmental stewardship is emphasized, with student-teachers learning about sustainable practices and the importance of preserving natural resources. This education prepares them to instill a sense of responsibility towards the environment in their future students, fostering a generation that values sustainability and community engagement. Through IKS, student-teachers become advocates for social justice and environmental care, preparing them to lead initiatives that benefit both their communities and the planet.

REACHING OUT TO THE COMMUNITY

Experiential learning is a cornerstone of the IKS approach, emphasizing hands-on, practical learning experiences that connect theory to real- life situations. At Rahul College of Education, this may include outdoor education, where student- teachers engage with nature and local ecosystems to understand Indigenous ways of knowing and interacting with the environment. Such experiences might also involve internships, fieldwork, or community-based projects that allow student-teachers to apply theoretical knowledge in authentic contexts. For example, they might work on developing culturally relevant lesson plans that incorporate local traditions and knowledge into their teaching. This hands-on approach not only enhances understanding but also cultivates skills such as critical thinking, adaptability, and problem-solving. As student- teachers engage in experiential learning, they are better prepared to create meaningful learning experiences for their future students, connecting academic content to students' lives and communities.

The incorporation of Indigenous Knowledge Systems at Rahul College of Education is a transformative educational philosophy that promotes holistic development, ethical and value- based learning, community and environmental responsibility, and experiential learning. By fostering these principles, the college prepares student-teachers to become reflective, empathetic, and socially responsible educators who are equipped to meet the diverse needs of their students and communities. This comprehensive approach not only enriches the student- teachers' personal and professional growth but also empowers them to contribute positively to society and the environment, creating a ripple effect of positive change in education and beyond. By incorporating IKS into its teacher education programs, Rahul College of Education aims to develop educators who are not only well-versed in modern pedagogies but are also grounded in traditional wisdom, enabling them to offer a more holistic education to their students.

Indian Knowledge Systems: Key Approaches

One of the key aspects of IKS is the practice of Yoga and Meditation, which focuses on the holistic development of the individual. At Rahul College of Education, these practices are integrated into the daily routine of student-teachers to promote mental clarity, emotional balance, and physical well-being. Yoga and meditation sessions are not just viewed as physical exercises but are seen as methods to foster self-awareness, mindfulness, and inner calm—qualities that are essential for effective teaching. For example, every morning, student-teachers participate in a yoga session that includes asanas (postures) and pranayama (breathing exercises), followed by a meditation session. This practice helps them manage stress, improve concentration, and develop patience and empathy—skills that are crucial in the teaching profession.Value-based education is a core component of Indian Knowledge Systems. At Rahul College of Education, the focus is on inculcating values such as compassion, humility, integrity, and respect for diversity in student-teachers. These values are drawn from ancient Indian texts like the Vedas, Upanishads, Bhagavad Gita, and Jain and Buddhist philosophies.For instance, student-teachers are encouraged to study excerpts from the Bhagavad Gita, which emphasize ethical action (karma), selflessness, and the importance of doing one's duty without attachment to the results. They discuss how these principles can be applied to their future roles as educators—fostering a sense of responsibility towards their students and society at large.

Workshops on Indian Ethics are also conducted, where educators explore moral dilemmas and the importance of ethics in teaching. These discussions help student-teachers internalize the values that are at the heart of effective and ethical teaching practices. **Storytelling** has been a traditional method of imparting knowledge in Indian education. Stories from the **Ramayana**, **Mahabharata**, **Panchatantra**, and **Jataka Tales** have long been used to teach moral lessons and societal values. At Rahul College of Education, storytelling is used as a pedagogical tool to teach not only ethical values but also to enhance communication skills, creativity, and imagination in future teachers. For example, in a module on **Value Education**, student-teachers analyze stories from the **Mahabharata** to explore themes like leadership, justice, and moral conflict. These discussions encourage critical thinking and provide student-teachers with examples they can use in their own classrooms to convey complex moral and ethical issues in an accessible way.

At Rahul College of Education, the philosophies of great Indian educators such as Mahatma Gandhi, Rabindranath Tagore, Swami Vivekananda, and Sri Aurobindo are studied and incorporated into modern teaching methods. These philosophers emphasized experiential learning, holistic education, and the integration of spiritual and moral development in education. For instance, Gandhian education focused on Nai Talim (Basic Education), which integrates intellectual, physical, and manual work to promote self-reliance and moral development. Student-teachers at Rahul College of Education explore how these principles can be applied to modern classrooms, encouraging students to engage in hands-on learning while developing practical life skills.Similarly, Tagore's philosophy of education emphasized the importance of creativity, freedom, and a connection to nature. Student-teachers are encouraged to create lesson plans that integrate creative arts, outdoor learning, and exploration, fostering a sense of wonder and curiosity in their future students.Drawing from the rich tradition of Ayurveda, the ancient Indian system of medicine, Rahul College of Education incorporates principles of holistic health and environmental education into its curriculum. Student-teachers learn about the Ayurvedic principles of balance and sustainability, which are directly connected to environmental responsibility.For example, in environmental education classes, student-teachers are introduced to Ayurvedic concepts such as the doshas (biological energies) and their connection to the natural elements. They learn how to teach students about the importance of maintaining harmony with nature and the impact of human activities on the environment. Workshops on sustainable living practices, such as organic farming and waste management, are also conducted, providing student-teachers with practical examples they can bring into their classrooms.

Indian Knowledge Systems place a significant emphasis on the **arts** as a means of learning. **Indian classical music, dance, and art** are viewed as pathways to understanding deeper philosophical truths and developing emotional intelligence. At Rahul College of Education, the arts are integrated into interdisciplinary learning, helping student-teachers connect academic content with creative expression.For example, in a course on **cultural education**, student-teachers explore how **ragas** (musical scales in Indian classical music) can be used to evoke emotions and moods in the classroom. They learn to use music as a tool to calm students, enhance focus, or stimulate creativity. Similarly, student-teachers engage with Indian **folk arts** and **crafts** to understand how these traditional practices can be used to teach history, social studies, and even science. India has a rich history of contributions to mathematics and science, with scholars like **Aryabhata, Brahmagupta, Bhaskaracharya**, and others making ground breaking discoveries in fields such as algebra, astronomy, and geometry. At Rahul College of Education, student-teachers are introduced to these contributions as part of their training in mathematics and science education. For instance, while studying mathematical pedagogy, student-teachers explore ancient Indian concepts like **Vedic mathematics**, which offers simple techniques for complex calculations. They learn how to incorporate these methods into their teaching to make mathematics more accessible and enjoyable for students.

In science education, student-teachers study **ancient Indian advancements** in fields such as metallurgy, medicine, and astronomy. They reflect on how these contributions can be integrated into their teaching to inspire a sense of pride in India's scientific heritage while promoting critical thinking and innovation in their students.Indian Knowledge Systems emphasize the importance of community and social responsibility. At Rahul College of Education, student-teachers engage in **community-based learning** projects that encourage them to apply their knowledge in real-world settings, fostering a sense of **social responsibility** and **service**.For example, student-teachers participate in **service-learning projects** where they work with local communities to address issues such as education for underprivileged children, environmental conservation, and health awareness. These projects provide student-teachers with valuable hands-on experience while reinforcing the IKS principles of compassion, selflessness, and community engagement.

Learning through Indian Knowledge Systems (IKS) at Rahul College of Education offers a transformative educational experience for student-teachers. This approach not only enriches their understanding of educational theories but also cultivates a well-rounded and culturally enriched identity. Learning through IKS promotes holistic development, which is essential for student-teachers as they prepare to become educators. This holistic approach encompasses intellectual, emotional, physical, and spiritual growth. By engaging with various dimensions of knowledge—ranging from traditional sciences like Ayurveda and yoga to philosophical concepts—student-teachers develop a balanced perspective on life. This balance equips them with greater empathy, emotional intelligence, and resilience, qualities that are essential for effective teaching. As they learn to integrate these aspects into their lives, they become more attuned to their students' diverse needs, creating a supportive and nurturing classroom environment. Holistic development fosters a sense of well-being and personal growth, allowing student-teachers to become more relatable and compassionate educators.

Integrating ethical principles from IKS into the curriculum helps student-teachers become more mindful of their responsibilities as educators and role models. IKS emphasizes values such as respect, compassion, integrity, and social responsibility, which are critical in the field of education. As student-teachers engage with these values, they develop a deeper understanding of their role in shaping young minds. They learn the importance of ethical decision-making and the impact of their actions on their students and communities. This ethical grounding not only influences their teaching practices but also inspires them to model these values for their students. By fostering a value-based approach to education, student-teachers are better prepared to create inclusive and equitable learning environments that promote respect for diversity and social justice.

Learning through IKS fosters cultural awareness and pride among student-teachers. By exploring the richness of India's cultural and intellectual traditions—such as classical literature, philosophy, art, and folklore—student-teachers develop a strong sense of identity and connection to their heritage. This cultural appreciation is essential for educators, as it empowers them to teach their students about the importance of cultural diversity and the value of preserving traditional knowledge. Student-teachers can draw upon these rich traditions in their own teaching practices, helping to instill a sense of pride and appreciation for Indian heritage in their future students. As they celebrate and share their cultural roots, they contribute to the broader narrative of cultural continuity and resilience, ensuring that these invaluable traditions are passed down to future generations.

IKS emphasizes experiential and hands-on learning, allowing student-teachers to engage with real-world problems and develop practical solutions. This approach contrasts sharply with rote learning, fostering critical thinking, creativity, and problem-solving skills. Student-teachers might participate in fieldwork, community projects, or traditional practices that provide them with firsthand experience and insight into the applications of IKS. For instance, they may learn about local crafts, sustainable farming practices, or traditional healing methods, which enhance their understanding of how knowledge is constructed and applied in everyday life. This experiential learning helps student-teachers connect theoretical concepts to practical applications, making their education more relevant and impactful. It also equips them with the skills to create engaging learning experiences for their own students, bridging the gap between theory and practice in the classroom. Through the study of disciplines like Ayurveda and other IKS traditions, student-teachers learn the importance of sustainability and living in harmony with nature. IKS emphasizes a deep respect for the environment and highlights the interconnectedness of all living beings. Student- teachers explore traditional ecological knowledge, understanding sustainable practices that have been passed down through generations. This knowledge encourages them to promote environmental stewardship in their future classrooms, teaching their students about responsible consumption, conservation, and the significance of protecting natural resources. By integrating sustainability principles into their teaching, student-teachers can inspire future generations to adopt eco-friendly practices, fostering a sense of responsibility towards the planet and encouraging active participation in environmental conservation.

EPILOGUE

At Rahul College of Education, learning through Indian Knowledge Systems provides a unique, holistic approach to teacher education that bridges the gap between traditional wisdom and modern pedagogy. By integrating the philosophical, ethical, and practical elements of IKS into the curriculum, Rahul College of Education equips future educators with the tools they need to create meaningful, value-based, and impactful learning experiences for their students. In doing so, it ensures that the next generation of teachers is not only competent in contemporary educational practices but also deeply rooted in the timeless wisdom of India's rich intellectual traditions.

References:

- Jain, M.P. (2019). *Indian Knowledge System and Education. Indian Journal of Traditional Knowledge*, 18(4), 600-605.
- Kapur, M., & Prabhu, R. (2017). *Indian Knowledge Systems and Mental Health.* Springer.
- Radhakrishnan, S. (1994). *The Principal Upanishads.* HarperCollins Publishers India.

www.ingramcontent.com/pod-product-compliance
Lightning Source LLC
LaVergne TN
LVHW070943160826
845679LV00022B/1897

9798896104681